BIRD TALK
and Other Stories
by Xu Xu

BIRD TALK
and Other Stories
by Xu Xu

Modern Tales of a Chinese Romantic

Translated and with commentary
by Frederik H. Green

Stone Bridge Press • *Berkeley, California*

Published by
Stone Bridge Press
P. O. Box 8208, Berkeley, CA 94707
tel 510-524-8732 • sbp@stonebridge.com • www.stonebridge.com

10 9 8 7 6 5 4 3 2 1   2023 2022 2021 2020

p-isbn 978-1-61172-055-6 (paperback)
p-isbn 978-1-61172-059-4 (hardcover)
e-isbn 978-1-61172-939-9 (ebook)

Contents

Acknowledgments

This book has been many years in the making. Consequently, it has accrued many a debt of gratitude. I chanced upon Xu Xu and his short story "Ghost Love" while combing through Republican-period journals at Yale's Sterling Memorial Library for a graduate seminar with Charles Laughlin, my first doctoral advisor. My chance encounter with Xu Xu turned into a dissertation whose completion was supervised by Jing Tsu, my second advisor. Both have been equally inspiring and caring mentors. Chris Hill was most generous with time, advice, and criticism, and Kang-I Sun Chang always shared my enthusiasm for Xu Xu. Many years ago, Susan Daruvala watered my budding interest in modern Chinese literature while Joe McDermott was the one who sent me on the road to romanticism. The late P. K. Leung welcomed me to Lingnan University in Hong Kong and provided encouragement and guidance. Lo Wai-luen shared anecdotes about her former teacher Xu Xu as well as some treasured first editions. Y. M. Bow and his sister Bow Sui May Hidemi were the most wonderful and generous hosts. In Shanghai, my thanks go to Chen Zishan and to Gao Bo and Xiong Di.

Work on the book got started in earnest with the help of a Junior Scholar Grant from the Chiang Ching-kuo Foundation. Most of the early drafts of the translations in this book were completed in a carrel at the Center for Chinese Studies (CCS) during a three-month residency at the National Central Library

(NCL) in Taipei in 2015, made possible through a Taiwan Fellowship from the Ministry of Foreign Affairs of the Republic of China. I polished up my translations and wrote the Introduction and Afterword during a subsequent stay at the CCS in 2018. I will forever be grateful to the wonderful staff of the CCS and NCL who made me feel so welcome in their library. In Taiwan, Liu T'ie-hu and Chung Shao-Chih helped me see clearly whenever I got stuck with a difficult text passage, and Shie Shrtzung and Nikky Lin provided mental (and culinary) support. Lin Ying-chih patiently listened when I told him why Xu Xu needed to be translated, and Jimmy Liao knew it all along. Ch'en Pao-ling and her family took me to Mount Ali so that we could look for the all-souls tree. We did not find it, but instead we saw the morning sunrise.

My colleague Chris Wen-chao Li at SFSU helped me with the trickiest of translation problems. Ilana Wistinetzki was the first to read the entire manuscript, with a red pen in hand. Jennifer Feeley offered invaluable feedback after reading drafts of all the stories and the Introduction. Jianye He of the Berkeley Starr Library went out of her way to help me find the most obscure of materials. My colleagues Charles Egan, Yang Xiao-Desai, Josephine Tsao, April Phung, Hsin-Yun Liu, and Mia Segura in the Chinese Program at SFSU provided cheers and feedback along the way, as did Wei Yang Menkus and Stephen Roddy across town at USF. Chuen-fung Wong always believed in this book and kept encouraging me. Constantine Rusanov has made me a better writer, and was always there when I needed him most. Mark Levine was never more than a phone call away, and Peter Hegedus never more than an email.

Joe Allen, Mark and Jean Barnekow, Xiaomei Chen, Clare Cheng, William Coker, Maghiel van Crevel, Melissa Dale, Paul van Els, Victor Fan, Howard Goldblatt, Kendall Heitzman, Amanda Hsu, Roland Hsu, Junliang Huang, Andrew Jones, Milton Katz, Lucas Klein, Jon von Kowallis, Karl Kwan, Jim Laine,

Haiyan Lee, Hua Li, Luo Liang, Sylvia Li-chun Lin, Andrea Lingenfelter, Chris Lupke, Lois Lyles, David Martyn, Jason McGrath, Kitty Millet, Thomas Moran, Kenny Ng, Li Li Peters, Steve Riep, Rosemary Roberts, Haun Saussy, Chris Scott, Chris Song, Brian Steininger, Satoko Suzuki, Andy Tsai, Doris Tseng, Sebastian Veg, Ban Wang, Ya Wang, Brett Wilson, Shengqing Wu, Edith Yang, Xin Yang, Zhiyi Yang, Christina Yee, and Yanhong Zhu have all at some point read or listened to parts of this project and generously shared comments and criticism.

Peter Goodman has been the most wonderful of editors who first patiently waited for the manuscript and then speedily put it to print. Special thanks go to Fiametta Yin Peh Hsu and Yin-chiu Hsu, for trusting me with the task of translating parts of their late father's literary legacy, and to my "brother" Frederik Schodt for his good humor and encouragement over the years. Finally, I want to thank my wife Miwa for (almost never) minding the long hours I spent with Xu Xu instead of with her and for being just as enthusiastic about this project as I have been. All of you, I would like to thank from the bottom of my heart.

—*FHG*

INTRODUCTION
Xu Xu's Literary Journey through Twentieth-Century China

The five short stories collected in this anthology along with the critical essay at the end of this volume offer a glance at the literary legacy of Xu Xu 徐訏 (1908–80), a Chinese writer who enjoyed tremendous popularity throughout the late 1930s and 1940s, prior to leaving China for Hong Kong in 1950. In Hong Kong, Xu Xu continued to write copious amounts of fiction, as well as poetry, drama, essays, and literary criticism. His collected works that were published in Taiwan between 1966 and 1970 consist of fifteen volumes.[1] Xu Xu also edited several literary journals and taught Chinese literature at a number of colleges and universities, eventually chairing the Chinese Department at Hong Kong Baptist University until his death in 1980. Through his work as a writer, critic, and scholar, Xu Xu had a considerable impact on a new generation of writers and scholars that emerged in postwar Hong Kong and Taiwan.

Spanning a period of some thirty years, from 1937 until 1965, the five short stories also offer the reader an unusual glimpse into China's turbulent twentieth century. The ways in which Xu Xu responded through his fiction to China's ideological upheavals of the 1920s and 1930s, the War of Resistance against Japan, the ensuing bitter civil war that led to the founding of the People's Republic of China in 1949 and the Nationalists' retreat to Taiwan, and finally his own exile in Hong Kong are, in many respects, unique and at times put him at odds with his contemporaries. In the 1930s, when many progressive intellectuals supported the leftist cause, Xu Xu embraced a distinctly cosmopolitan liberalism. During the war years, when both the political left and right espoused patriotic and nationalist narratives that celebrated collective action, Xu Xu's fiction and drama explored quasi-existentialist themes and pursued individualism. Finally, in 1950, Xu Xu left the newly founded People's Republic, not for Nationalist Taiwan but for Hong Kong. Unwilling to align himself with either of the two authoritarian postwar regimes, Xu Xu decided to remain in colonial Hong Kong, a city he never entirely embraced as his home. Yet it was also in Hong Kong where, unhindered by ideological constraints, he produced some of his most significant literary works. As I will discuss in more detail in the essay at the back of this volume, it was also during his exile in Hong Kong that his distinct literary aesthetics matured, placing him in the proximity of Western twentieth-century neo-romantic artists, such as Hermann Hesse, and connecting his work to a global literary modernity. These neo-romantic tendencies are nowhere more discernible than in his short story "Bird Talk" 鳥語, the title story of this collection.

* * *

Xu Xu was born into a gentry family in Cixi near Ningbo in the coastal province of Zhejiang during the last years of the Qing dynasty (1644–1912). His given name was Xu Boyu 徐伯訏, and he later adopted the first and last characters of his given name as his pen name. The character 訏 can be pronounced both as "Xu" or "Yu," and while Xu Xu himself preferred the latter pronunciation, the former eventually prevailed, especially in America, where he entered the catalog of the Library of Congress as "Xu Xu." Like many of his peers, Xu Xu received an early education that was steeped in classical Chinese learning, but he was also exposed to modern schooling and Western ideas that became more widely accepted during the last years of the Qing dynasty and the early Republican period (1912–49).

In 1927, Xu Xu was admitted to Peking University, which was then the country's leading center for progressive social and political ideas. Xu Xu majored in philosophy and developed a lasting interest in the ideas of Henri Bergson, the French philosopher who had won the Nobel Prize in Literature in 1927 and whose writings on intuition and creativity not only had a profound impact on the literary works of European modernists such as Marcel Proust and Virginia Woolf but also on Xu Xu's fictional oeuvre. Following his graduation in 1931, Xu Xu went on to study psychology for two additional years before moving to Shanghai in 1933 to begin his literary career under the auspices of Lin Yutang 林語堂 (1895–1976), the well-known polyglot writer and critic who ran a number of successful publishing ventures.

Xu Xu became a member of Lin Yutang's Analects Group 論語派, a loose circle of like-minded liberal and cosmopolitan intellectuals, and worked as editor for two of the group's journals, namely the bimonthlies *The Analects* 論語 and *This Human World* 人間世. Both journals published predominantly prose essays, or *xiaopinwen* 小品文, a genre that Lin Yutang was actively promoting and that many of the group's writers excelled at. Often humorous in nature, these essays presented social commentaries that were an alternative to the increasingly politicized and polemical writings of leftist intellectuals. Xu Xu, in those early years, wrote mostly free-verse poetry but also contributed his own essays that typically commented on cultural differences between China and the West, a topic that was of great interest to readers in Shanghai and Republican-period China.

Shanghai in the 1930s had grown into China's foremost

metropolis. The country's industrial and commercial center and also its publishing hub, it was a city known for its cosmopolitan culture. In the wake of the first Opium War (1839–42), a foreign settlement had sprung up on the lands north of the walled Chinese city, and it gradually developed into the Anglo-American International Settlement and the French Concession, semi-colonial and largely self-governed territories at the heart of the rapidly expanding city (see map on pages 120–21).

While the foreign concessions were a constant reminder of Western imperialism in China, they also provided the city with many modern amenities, such as movie theaters, department stores, dance halls, and nightclubs. There were also horse- and dog-racing tracks as well as Western-style cafés and bookstores selling Western-language books. In addition, there were two prestigious universities, the Anglican St. John's University that had been founded by American missionaries (Lin Yutang was one of its graduates) and the Jesuit Université l'Aurore located in the French Concession. While political repression and strict censorship were a daily reality in China during the Republican period, Shanghai's foreign concessions, because of their extra-territorial status, offered a considerable degree of freedom to Chinese writers and intellectuals, who moved there in increasing numbers.

By the time Xu Xu arrived in Shanghai, Chiang Kai-shek and his Nationalist KMT party had united China after years of warlordism and had moved the capital from Beijing to Nanjing. Informally referred to as the Nanjing Decade, the period that lasted from 1927 to 1937 was characterized by relative stability and economic growth. However, it was also bracketed by two traumatic events of lasting historic significance. On April 12, 1927, Chiang Kai-shek betrayed his former Communist allies and ordered the violent purge of Chinese Communist Party (CCP) organizations in Shanghai and later all over KMT-controlled China. The Shanghai Massacre or April 12 Incident, as it is also known, ushered in the first phase of the civil war between the CCP and the KMT and ultimately shifted the CCP's base of support from the urban proletariat to the countryside. Chiang Kai-shek might well have succeeded with his campaign to eradicate Chinese Communism had it not been for Japan's aggressive expansionism that, on July 7, 1937, eventually led to full-fledged warfare between China and Japan.

Like many intellectuals of his generation, especially those studying at Peking University, Xu Xu had briefly become interested in Communism, but his interests soon shifted to aesthetics, and his political views were more aligned with those of the liberal Lin Yutang and other less radical members of the Analects Group. This is not to say that Xu Xu or the members of the Analects Group remained indifferent to the political situation around them. Especially Lin Yutang often criticized the KMT's proto-fascism and mocked their censorship laws. In September 1935, Lin Yutang established the bimonthly *Celestial Winds* 宇宙風, a broad-ranging and well-received literary magazine that also covered current affairs and provided social commentaries. One year later, in September 1936, Lin Yutang, together with Tao Kangde 陶亢德 and the brothers Huang Jiade 黃嘉德 and Huang Jiayin 黃嘉音, established *West Wind* 西風, a journal equally broad in scope but that in addition focused on international affairs, such as Japanese imperialism and fascism in Europe.

Xu Xu's interests during those years were not limited to literature but included the arts in general as well as social sciences and psychology. To give voice to his many interests, Xu Xu, together with Sun Chenghe 孫成和, had in early 1936 co-launched the short-lived semimonthly *Heaven, Earth, and Man* 天地人 that published articles on a wide variety of topics such as Western dance, architecture, behaviorism, folk songs, Abyssinian literature, and painting. Probably its most important contribution to Chinese literature was the first serialization of a Chinese translation of D. H. Lawrence's *Lady Chatterley's*

Lover. Xu Xu had also been invited to co-edit *Celestial Winds* and *West Wind*, but by then he had already decided to embark on study abroad in Paris. He did, however, agree to contribute essays about his experiences abroad to the newly established journals.

And so, in the fall of 1936, Xu Xu embarked on the Italian steamer *Conte Verde* of the Lloyd Triestino line for his journey to Europe. During his month-long crossing, Xu Xu composed numerous essays in which he wittily or caustically commented on cultural differences between the Chinese and the other ethnic groups he encountered, such as overseas Chinese, Indians, and Europeans. Many of these essays subsequently appeared in the pages of *Celestial Winds* and *West Wind*. His ensuing sojourn in Louvain, Belgium, for language study and later in Paris, where he enrolled in classes in philosophy at the Sorbonne, further inspired him to write a number of short stories and novellas that likewise appeared in the journals of the Analects Group. Works like "The Studio at Montparnasse" 蒙擺拿斯的畫室 and *The Gypsy Enticement* 吉布賽的誘惑 mostly explored romantic encounters between a confident Chinese first-person narrator (who typically resembled the young Xu Xu himself) and various European women. These short stories generally displayed a lyrical exoticism that, along with the worldly first-person narrator, became the hallmark of Xu Xu's early fiction.

It was also in the pages of the Analects Group's journal *Celestial Winds* that Xu Xu's short story "Ghost Love" 鬼戀, the opening story of this anthology, first appeared. Written just before his departure for Europe, "Ghost Love" was published in two installments in the January issues of 1937 and became an instant success. Xu Xu later revised the original and published it in the form of a book, which by 1949 had gone through nineteen print runs and had gained Xu Xu the moniker 鬼才 or "ghostly genius" (my translation is based on the original 1937 version). It was also adapted for the screen in 1941 and then again in 1956 and 1995.

"Ghost Love" is a modern gothic tale set in 1930s Shanghai

in which a first-person narrator relates his encounter with a mysterious woman who claims to be a ghost. Meeting one night at a tobacco store on Nanjing Road, Shanghai's main shopping street, the two start a liaison that lasts for over a year. The reader accompanies the two on their nightly strolls through Shanghai, whose geography often played an important role in urban fiction of the Republican period. While the narrator in "Ghost Love" frequently references traditional Chinese ghost stories, the story is intrinsically modern and a testimony to urban cosmopolitanism in prewar Shanghai. The mysterious ghost-woman wears a *qipao*, the tight-fitting dress that was popularized by Chinese socialites in Shanghai during the 1920s and 1930s, smokes a popular British cigarette brand, and is extremely knowledgeable about both Western and Chinese cultures. She also speaks several languages and later reveals that she is the daughter of a Jewish mother and an overseas Chinese father. While "Ghost Love" also touches upon the revolutionary struggles of the 1920s and the violence that had ensued after Chiang Kai-shek's betrayal of his Communist allies in Shanghai, the story is largely skeptical of collective action and ideological narratives and essentially individualistic in nature.

In fact, most of Xu Xu's fiction of those years, especially the short stories produced during his sojourn in Europe, is characterized by an exoticism that remains in large part aloof from politics and concerns itself more with questions of aesthetics and literary style. Written during his passage to Europe aboard the *Conte Verde* in August 1936 and serialized in *The Eastern Miscellany* 東方雜誌 later that year, his short story "The Goddess of the Arabian Sea" 阿拉伯海的女神, for example, describes the encounter onboard a steamer between a first-person narrator and a beautiful Arab woman who claims to be a sorceress. When she tells him a tale of a young goddess who roams the waters they are passing through, the narrator excitedly declares, "I want to pursue all artistic fantasies, because their beauty to me is reality," and then announces that "in this world there are people who pursue dreams of the real, while I seek out the real within dreams."[2]

The narrator here appears to echo Bergsonian concepts of intuition that provide an artist with the impetus to seek for truths and realities beyond the purely mimetic and that continued to shape Xu Xu's fictional worlds. Not surprising, the narrator in "The Goddess of the Arabian Sea" eventually meets and falls in love with the goddess, only to be brought back to reality when he awakens in his deckchair, drenched by a big wave. Illusion and reality are similarly interwoven in the novella *The Absurd English Channel* 荒謬的英法海峽 from 1939 in which a first-person narrator is kidnapped by pirates during a crossing from France to England and brought to a utopian island state. Despite voicing some veiled criticism of corruption in China and dismay over Soviet-style Communism and the Stalinist purges, the novella is foremost an exotic love story that comes to an abrupt end as the ferry docks in Dover and the narrator awakens from a dream.

* * *

Even though Xu Xu largely refrained from commenting on the political realities in China in his fiction of those years, politics eventually caught up with him while studying in Paris. Following Japan's invasion of China proper in the summer of 1937, many Chinese students studying abroad felt compelled to return home to show their support of the Chinese War of Resistance. This situation presented Xu Xu with a real personal dilemma, because he appears to have fallen in love with a Japanese classmate. Named Asabuki Tomiko 朝吹登水子 (1917–2005), this classmate would herself become a well-known novelist in postwar Japan, and their short-lived romance would eventually find its way into her autobiographical novel *The Other Side of Love* 愛のむこう側.

In her novel, a tall, handsome, and poetically inclined young man named Yu falls on his knees near the entrance to the Parc

Montsouris in Paris's fourteenth arrondissement in the early fall of 1937 and declares his love to his Japanese classmate, asking her to marry him and to accompany him back to China. She politely declines, reminding him of the impossibility of his request in the face of Japan's invasion of his homeland. The young man then gets up, looks at her one last time, and disappears into the night. The following day, he takes a train to Marseille and embarks on a steamer back to Shanghai.[3]

Xu Xu himself never explicitly wrote about this episode, and we have no way of verifying Asabuki's fictionalized account of their short liaison. The episode is nevertheless insightful, as it suggests that, for Xu Xu, the outbreak of war constituted not only a crisis of a national dimension but also a personal crisis that resulted in moral and emotional conflicts. While most progressive writers depicted the conflict as a clear dichotomy between aggressor and victim and frequently focused on the cruelty of the Japanese invader and the heroism of the Chinese resistance, Xu Xu subsequently explored the more abstract moral dilemmas and personal tragedies caused by war. This is particularly visible in his wartime drama. In his five-act play *Brothers* 兄弟 from 1942, for example, two estranged half-brothers suddenly face each other on opposite sides of the conflict. The younger brother is a guerilla fighting the invader, while the older is a high-ranking general of the Japanese army. When the older brother finds himself obliged to court-martial his younger brother after an attack on a train, a tragedy of Shakespearean dimensions unfolds, sparked by the conflict over personal versus national allegiances.[4]

The human tragedy of war is also explored in another popular short story that Xu Xu wrote shortly after arriving in Paris and that is included in this anthology. In "The Jewish Comet" 猶太的彗星 from 1937, a first-person narrator named Xu travels to Europe aboard an Italian steamer and falls in love with a Jewish secret agent who is fighting fascism in the Spanish Civil War. Like *Brothers*, "The Jewish Comet" ends tragically, foreshadowing the catastrophe that was already looming over Europe. While the plot is driven by a similar mix of mystery and exoticism seen in many of Xu Xu's prewar short stories, "The Jewish Comet" also bespeaks the interest cosmopolitan readers in Shanghai took in European politics and in the plight of the Jews in particular.

The Jewish struggle for a homeland has featured in the imagination of Chinese intellectuals since at least the end of the Qing dynasty, allowing for ready identification with tales of national suffering but also bearing the potential to heighten Chinese readers' own sense of nationalism and national survival. Xu Xu's choice of a Jewish heroine fighting in the Spanish Civil War is not bereft of historical likelihood. A sizable portion of the volunteers fighting in the International Brigade were, in fact, Jews. Jews also formed a considerable contingent of foreigners living in Shanghai, some of whom were Baghdadi Jews who had come with the British following the Opium Wars; others were Russian Jews who had fled their homeland following the October Revolution and the subsequent civil war. In the wake of Hitler's rise in Germany, and especially following the violent anti-Semitic attacks of the Night of Broken Glass (Kristallnacht) of 1938, Shanghai further saw an influx of some 18,000 European Jews who fled ever harsher persecution in Germany and the territories that would soon fall under German control. Since the International Settlement did not require a visa for arriving visitors, Shanghai became one of the last safe havens for Jews desperate to leave Europe. Incidentally, the Italian Lloyd Triestino steamers *Conte Verde* and *Conte Rosso*, sailing from ports in Nazi Germany's axis partner Italy, played a crucial role in helping many of them reach Shanghai.

By the time Xu Xu returned to Shanghai from Europe in late 1937, the city was occupied by Japanese forces. Only the International Settlement and the French Concession remained neutral territory, forming what came to be known as the "solitary island"

孤島. Xu Xu resumed his editorship with the Analects Group's journals and continued to publish his exotic romances that proved very popular with the reading public. Only when the Japanese also occupied the International Settlement following the attack on Pearl Harbor (the French Concession had already lost its neutrality following Germany's invasion of France and had fallen under the jurisdiction of Vichy France) did he decide to leave the city for Chongqing, the Nationalists' wartime capital in the hinterland. Here, he wrote what is probably his best-known work of fiction, the wartime spy novel *The Rustling Wind* 風蕭蕭.

Set in Shanghai in the years leading up to Japan's attack on Pearl Harbor and related through the eyes of a cosmopolitan first-person narrator named Xu, *The Rustling Wind* is an epic tale of love and espionage that captured its reading audience through its vivid depiction of life in the foreign concessions and the promise of agency in the fight against the invader. By way of his liaisons with two enticing female secret agents and the beautiful daughter of an American army doctor, Xu the narrator unwittingly gets drawn into the web of wartime intelligence. However, with its many quasi-existentialist meditations on the meaning of friendship and beauty in times of war, *The Rustling Wind* retained a literariness that was absent from most other popular wartime works. *The Rustling Wind* was initially serialized in the wartime newspaper *Eradicator Daily* 掃蕩報 throughout 1943 and solidified Xu Xu's status as a national literary celebrity. It was subsequently turned into a movie and a TV series in Hong Kong and Taiwan in 1954 and the 1960s respectively, where it has continually remained in print.

Near the war's end, Xu Xu was sent to the US as a special envoy for *Eradicator Daily*. Upon his return to Shanghai in 1946, Xu Xu, with the help of Liu Yichang 劉以鬯 (1918–2018), resumed publication of his wartime works, many of which had previously only appeared in journals or newspapers. In 1949, Xu Xu got married and planned to settle in Ningbo with his wife and his son and daughter from a previous marriage. However, as Mao Zedong proclaimed the founding of the People's Republic in Beijing that year and Chiang Kai-shek's Nationalist government retreated to Taiwan after succumbing in the civil war that had resumed between the CCP and the KMT after Japan's capitulation, Xu Xu began to feel that his literary legacy might become a liability under the new regime.

* * *

Xu Xu had been attacked by leftist critics all throughout the 1930s for writing fiction that was deemed escapist at best and detrimental to their political cause at worst. Then, in 1945, an essay on "Ghost Love" appeared in a short volume of criticism by the young Marxist critic Shi Huaichi 石懷池 (1925–45?) that clearly revealed the incompatibility of Xu Xu's idealist aesthetics with the utilitarian role of art in Communist China. In the essay, Shi Huaichi condemned the corrupting and degenerating effects Xu Xu's work had on upright revolutionaries, claiming that

> it will invariably cause you to forget the cruel reality of the world … cause you to ignore the hideous scars our nation has received, and lead you to distance yourself from that cruel struggle between old and new that is currently being carried out all around us…. Instead, it will invite you to enter an illusionary world.

Shi then advised readers "to throw it into the cesspool."[5] It must have been criticism like this that compelled Xu Xu to board a train to Hong Kong in May of 1950, leaving behind his wife, who had just given birth to a daughter. Like many other writers who left the mainland in those years, Xu Xu mistakenly thought that his sojourn in Hong Kong would only be a temporary exile.

Accessing illusionary worlds and alternative spheres of reality had indeed become increasingly central to Xu Xu's literary quest. While the narrator in "Goddess of the Arabian Sea" had declared his unconditional surrender to artistic fantasies, he was nevertheless brought back to reality when he awoke from his dream. In his short story "Hallucination" 幻覺 published in 1947, however, the distinction between reality and illusion is altogether blurred. In "Hallucination," the story's narrator meets a painter who, whenever he gazes at one of his small oil paintings, is able to access his own past and temporarily relive the happiness he knew with his now deceased lover. Aware that his account might raise suspicion, the painter insists that "illusions and reality are very difficult to tell apart, for reality may consist of the common illusions of the majority, while an illusion can be one person's reality."[6] The deliberate blurring of illusion and reality as well as of the past and present not only echoes the philosophy of Henri Bergson that encouraged the artist to transform reality through art, it also signals a shift in Xu Xu's aesthetic concerns. No longer did his protagonists venture on exotic journeys to foreign lands; instead they embarked on quests to recapture irretrievably lost love or beauty they had known in bygone days. This nostalgic gesture became ever more pronounced in Xu Xu's postwar fiction from Hong Kong.

The short story "Bird Talk" from 1950 perfectly epitomizes Xu Xu's use of nostalgia in his postwar fiction. It allowed him to give voice to a real sense of loss that resulted from his physical exile in Hong Kong, brought about by the political changes that were shaping China and the world in the wake of World War II. At the same time it allowed him to explore a metaphysical homelessness that is bound up with the experience of modernity and that has driven many twentieth-century artists to reject a purely scientific depiction of reality and instead seek alternative realities within dreams or the fantastic.

"Bird Talk" is set in postwar Hong Kong, yet most of the story is narrated as a flashback that takes the reader to the pre-war Chinese countryside. Here, a first-person narrator from Shanghai encounters a shy and introverted girl who appears to be able to communicate with birds. Intrigued by her unusual talent, the narrator offers to school her in conventional subjects if she agrees to teach him bird language in return. His attempts at socializing her, however, are just as futile as her efforts at teaching him bird talk. The only subject the girl excels at is poetry. In fact, when reading poetry, she experiences the same sublime happiness as when she talks with birds. After the two are eventually separated, the narrator ends up in postwar Hong Kong, a city that has forever removed him from the pastoral idyll of the prewar Chinese countryside.

In "The All-Souls Tree" 百靈樹, the next work included in this anthology and another short story Xu Xu published not long after arriving in Hong Kong, the theme of physical exile is explored even more explicitly. Set in Taiwan after the Nationalists' retreat to the island, its topic is the death-defying love of a young couple separated on account of the civil war. The story relates a tragedy experienced by countless Chinese people affected by the political reality of the postwar world order, not least Xu Xu himself. At the same time, "The All-Souls Tree," along with his novella *The Other Shore* 彼岸 from 1951 that similarly delves into mythical and quasi-religious epiphanies, illustrates Xu Xu's aesthetic conviction that art that explores sublime or otherworldly experiences might offer some comfort to those grappling with the pain of loss and homesickness. Xu Xu himself remained separated from his wife and daughter in Shanghai, and the two eventually divorced when his wife's association with Xu Xu increasingly became a political liability. Xu Xu later remarried in Hong Kong and had a daughter with his third wife while his son of his first marriage settled in Taiwan.

* * *

In Hong Kong, Xu Xu continued to publish large amounts of fiction. In the period between 1950 and 1952 alone, he published twenty-one short stories and novellas. Most of these appeared in the literary supplement of the Hong Kong newspaper *Sing Tao Evening Post* 星島晚報. Buoyed by his prewar and wartime fame, Xu Xu remained popular with readers in Hong Kong, most of whom were refugees from the mainland like himself—by the end of 1950, almost two million refugees had arrived in Hong Kong from the mainland, and over the next two decades, several hundred thousand more would follow. As a result, living space was scarce and life in Hong Kong was far from easy. Conditions started to improve when, in the late 1950s, the colonial government began to invest in public housing. By the early 1960s, Hong Kong's economy had also improved, in part because of the development of light industry, particularly electronics. And while immigration policies were increasingly tightened, Hong Kong continued to represent for many mainland immigrants the dream of a better life.

Xu Xu explored this theme in "When Ah Heung Came to Gousing Road" 來高升路的一個女人, the last story in this anthology and one of Xu Xu's later works of fiction. First published in 1965, this Cinderella story describes the fate of Ah Heung, a young mainland woman who has only recently arrived in Hong Kong to work as a maid in a rich family's household on Gousing Road. Ah Heung and her three friends, two of whom, like herself, are recent immigrants, embody the hardworking and honest immigrant class that sought a brighter future in the Crown colony. Unlike most of Xu Xu's fiction from his Hong Kong period, "When Ah Heung Came to Gousing Road" is hopeful and future oriented, yet by celebrating traditional virtues such as friendship and loyalty, Xu Xu also appears to voice nostalgia for a set of values that increasingly appeared to belong to a bygone era.

With its lightheartedness and colloquial style, "When Ah Heung Came to Gousing Road" is arguably the work with the most popular appeal of all the short stories collected in this anthology. As such, it also gives us an indication of the changing nature of literature and art in Hong Kong. So-called Sky Fiction 天空小說—plot-driven popular fiction that was written to be performed on the radio—enjoyed tremendous popularity throughout the postwar period. This phenomenon was accompanied by the growth of Hong Kong's movie industry. Throughout the 1920s and 1930s, Shanghai had been the undisputed center of the Chinese movie industry. However, in the wake of the founding of the People's Republic, many of the studios and a good number of its most prominent stars left Shanghai for Hong Kong, which over time developed into Asia's movie capital. Many writers, Xu Xu included, had their works adapted for the screen or provided screenplays to satisfy the ever-growing demand for Hong Kong cinema.

About a dozen of Xu Xu's works were turned into movies by Hong Kong studios, starring some of the best-known actors of the time. As early as 1953, Kuang-chi Tu 屠光啓 had directed an adaptation of *The Rustling Wind* for Shaw Brothers Studio, Hong Kong's most prominent studio, starring Li Lihua 李麗華 and Chun Yen 嚴俊. In 1954, Xu Xu's novella *Blind Love* 盲戀 was adapted for the screen and directed by Evan Yang 易文, with Li Lihua, Lo Wei 羅維, and Peter Chen Ho 陳厚 in the lead roles. Also known as *Always in My Heart*, it is a tragic love story between a blind young woman and a gentle, extremely talented writer whose Quasimodo-like appearance has turned him into a recluse. When, following surgery, the young woman regains sight, their relationship is forever changed. Xu Xu had a cameo appearance in *Blind Love*, which opened with him reading out the story's manuscript to a circle of movie-star friends, all of whom then turn out to be part of the movie's actual cast.

In 1956, a remake of *In Love with a Ghost* followed, directed by Kuang-chi Tu and starring Li Lihua and Zhang Yang 張揚. In 1960, Richard Li Han-hsiang 李翰祥 directed *Rear Entrance* 後門, based on Xu Xu's 1953 short story of the same title about a childless couple that adopts a young girl who subsequently upturns their hitherto stable lives. Starring Butterfly Wu 胡蝶, Wang Yin 王引, and Felicia Oi-Ming Wong 王愛明, it won the Best Picture Award of the seventh Asian Film Festival in Tokyo in 1960. Finally, in 1973, Shaw Brothers adapted Xu Xu's epic bildungsroman *The River of Fury* 江湖行, an ambitious multi-volume novel written between 1956 and 1961 that chronicles the stations of life of a first-person narrator through the Republican period and the war years. Directed by Tseng-chai Chang 張曾澤 and starring Lily Ho 何莉莉, Danny Lee 李修賢, and Ku Feng 谷峰, it was turned into an eighty-minute martial arts adventure that focused on the action and some of the romance of the original but barely explored the protagonist's existentialist quests and unfulfilled yearning that characterize the original novel.

During his exile in Hong Kong, Xu Xu continued to follow as closely as was possible from across the border the cultural and political developments in mainland China. He witnessed with anguish how writers he had known before the war were victimized for having failed to meet the ever more elusive expectations of the new regime toward its writers and artists, or "art workers" 文藝工作者, as they were now called. He frequently commented on those developments in his many essays and newspaper columns written in Hong Kong, some of which will be discussed in the critical essay at the end of this volume. While Xu Xu never participated in the production of what has become known as Greenback Culture 綠背文化—anti-Communist literature commissioned and sponsored by the United States Information Service (USIS) in Hong Kong and elsewhere in Asia—he did write a number of works of fiction in the early 1960s that explored the consequences of regime change in China on the lives of select individuals.

In "Going to the Country" 下鄉, an enthusiastic journalist returns to his natal village for a reportage about the success of collectivization. Through the journalist's encounters with the villagers, the reader learns about arbitrary executions in the wake of the land reform and the sobering reality of the Great Leap Forward. These perfunctory revelations, however, stand in stark contrast to the journalist's ultimate report, which is a glowing eulogy to the new society. In "Escape" 逃亡, an equally enthusiastic protagonist, this time an engineer, eventually grows disillusioned and decides to flee the system, an act that he pays for with his life. Xu Xu's most ambitious work about life and politics in the People's Republic, however, was his novel *A Tragic Era* 悲慘的世紀, which was first serialized in Hong Kong in 1969. A dystopian love story set in a Communist state that contends with a revisionist and a capitalist state for control over their planet located in a distant solar system, *A Tragic Era* shared elements of Aldous Huxley's *Brave New World* and George Orwell's *1984* and explored the incompatibility of complete devotion to the Communist system with individual fulfillment and personal integrity. With its depiction of power struggles between competing political factions, nationally televised struggle sessions, and the eventual love suicide of the two protagonists, readers in Hong Kong and Taiwan would have unmistakably understood *A Tragic Era* as a commentary on the politicization of life in the early decades of the People's Republic and in particular the excesses of the Cultural Revolution that had begun in 1966 and only came to an end with Mao's death in 1976.

* * *

By the early 1970s, Xu Xu's fiction increasingly failed to resonate with a younger generation of Hong Kong and Taiwanese readers, especially those who were too young to recall life in prewar China or who were born after the war. Only a few of Xu Xu's works of fiction were actually set in Hong Kong, and many of those that were, like his novel *Time and Brightness* 時與光 from 1966, depicted restless narrators in search of love and beauty who considered Hong Kong as nothing more than a temporary home and who nostalgically gazed at life in prewar China. Some of the cinematic adaptations of Xu Xu's work resolved this disconnect with a younger audience by changing the setting of the narrative from prewar China in the novel to present-day Hong Kong, as happened in *Blind Love* and *Rear Entrance*. In the meantime, a younger generation of writers who had come of age in Hong Kong began to write fiction and poetry through which they asserted their Hong Kong roots and extolled the mundane beauty that could be found amidst Hong Kong's mushrooming tenement blocks.

In one of Xu Xu's last works of fiction, the short story "Inside the Garden" 園內 (also known as "Phantom" 魅影) published in 1968, the quest for love, the restless wandering, and the solace found in metaphysical encounters that characterized so much of his postwar fiction all coalesce. When a young man on his way to study in England gets stranded in Hong Kong, he becomes obsessed with a woman whom he frequently observes strolling inside a walled garden opposite the house of a friend where he is staying. His attempts at becoming acquainted with her, however, remain unanswered, and it is only in his dreams that the two meet. The young man finally departs for England, yet he cannot rid himself of the memory of the woman in the garden and eventually returns to Hong Kong. He resumes observing her during her walks in the garden and eventually musters the courage to ask his friend to act as go-between. Only then does his friend inform him that the young lady who used to live in the house opposite had died of heart disease six months earlier.

While none of Xu Xu's fiction of either the prewar or postwar period was available in China throughout the first three decades of the People's Republic, it remained popular among readers in Hong Kong and Taiwan as well as in Chinese communities throughout Asia and America, especially among readers who had left the mainland after 1949. In addition to fiction, Xu Xu also continued to write poetry that regularly appeared in literary supplements of Hong Kong or Taiwanese newspapers. Some of it was even set to popular music. Xu Xu further continued to shape the Chinese literary field in Hong Kong as an editor of a number of literary journals. In 1953, he established the journal *Humor* 幽默. In the same year, he set up a publishing house with Cao Juren 曹聚仁 and began publishing the semi-monthly *Hot Blast* 熱風. In 1957, Lin Yutang's former journal *The Analects* was revived in Hong Kong, and Xu Xu became the editor. In 1968, Xu Xu started the semimonthly *Style* 筆端 and in 1975 the monthly *The Seven Arts* 七藝. While some of these journals only enjoyed short printruns and had a limited circulation, they provided an important platform for the burgeoning community of writers in Hong Kong. At the same time, they often featured translations of Western or Japanese literature or essays on foreign cultural trends. Postwar Hong Kong in effect was at that time the only place in the Chinese-speaking world that enjoyed a free press and only limited censorship, and Xu Xu, with his cosmopolitan outlook and broad interests in the arts, greatly facilitated the influx of new ideas.

Xu Xu also remained active as a cultural and literary critic. He regularly contributed essays on various topics ranging from Chinese politics to American literature to newspapers in Hong Kong and Taiwan. He also published several collections of essays that focused broadly on freedom and individualism and the function and role of art in society. Toward the end of his life, he began work on a history of modern Chinese literature, parts of which were posthumously published under the title *Taking a Glance at Modern Chinese Literature* 現代中國文學過眼錄. Equally important was his role as a teacher of a whole generation of writers and critics. Xu Xu taught Chinese literature at the Zhuhai College 珠海書院 and New Asia College 新亞書院 in Hong Kong and had teaching stints in Singapore and India before becoming professor and chair of the Chinese Department at Hong Kong Baptist University 香港浸會大學 in 1968. He remained there until his death from lung cancer in 1980, having assumed the position of Dean of the School of Literature in 1977.

Not long after Xu Xu's passing, his works, along with those of Lin Yutang and many other previously banned writers, became available again to readers in mainland China for the first time in more than three decades. During the 1980s, China embarked on a path to economic liberalization and experienced a decade-long cultural blossoming. Usually referred to as Culture Fever 文化熱, this period was characterized by openness to Western cultural imports and the rehabilitation and rediscovery of artists and critics who had been purged from the literary canon of the People's Republic. Xu Xu's cosmopolitanism, his liberal political stance, his individualism, and his critical interest in East-West cultural encounters as well as the exoticism of his prewar works all greatly appealed to readers and scholars who had experienced decades of political extremism and antagonism toward the West.

The Chinese scholar Yan Jiayan 嚴家炎 was the first to assign a certain romantic tendency to Xu Xu's work in the preface to his 1986 *Anthology of Modern Chinese Schools of Fiction* 中國現代各流派小説選. In his *History of Modern Chinese Schools of Fiction* 中國現代小説流派史 that followed in 1989, Yan paired Xu Xu's works with those of Wumingshi 無名氏 (1917–2002), another wartime writer whose aesthetics were characterized by cosmopolitanism, exoticism, and romance.[7] These writers' aesthetics, it appeared, had defied the mainstream narrative of nationalism and revolutionary radicalism in the 1930s and 1940s and now offered inspiration to mainland intellectuals who, after years of enforced ideological conformity, saw the chance for a cultural reawakening. Unfortunately, some of these hopes were dashed by the Tiananmen Massacre of June 4, 1989, in whose wake the CCP tightened control over cultural production and consumption.

Xu Xu's literary legacy, however, has continued to generate interest in China. Since the 1990s, a number of Chinese publishers have released books of his fiction, essays, plays, and poetry. In 1995, the filmmaker Chen Yifei 陳逸飛 produced a remake of "Ghost Love" entitled *Evening Liaison* 人約黃昏. In 2008, in commemoration of the one-hundredth anniversary of Xu Xu's birth, his complete works in sixteen volumes were published in Shanghai.[8] More recently, two different theatrical productions based on "Ghost Love" were staged in Shanghai and Hong Kong respectively, and the Shanghai author Wang Anyi 王安憶 wrote a play based on *The Rustling Wind*. Several studies of Xu Xu's works have appeared in China and Hong Kong over the past two decades, and a comprehensive biography was published by the scholars Wu Yiqin 吳義勤 and Wang Suxia 王素霞 in 2008.[9] My PhD dissertation on Xu Xu from 2009 is still the only comprehensive author study of Xu Xu in English,[10] but in 2019 a study by Christopher Rosenmeier that discusses some of Xu Xu and Wumingshi's prewar and wartime works in English was published in the UK.[11]

* * *

I hope that these five short stories as well as my critical essay at the end of this volume will provide a glimpse of this fascinating artist's career that spanned a large part of China's turbulent twentieth century. I would be humbled if my translations of "Bird Talk" and the other stories in this collection spoke to the reader in the way they have spoken to me, and delighted if they inspired others to seek out more of Xu Xu's literary works.

Endnotes

1. Xu Xu 徐訏. *Xu Xu quanji* 徐訏全集 [The complete works of Xu Xu]. Volumes 1–15. Taipei: Zhengzhong shuju, 1966.

2. Xu Xu 徐訏. *Xu Xu wenji* 徐訏文集 [The collected works of Xu Xu], edited by Qian Zhenhua 錢震華. Volumes 1–16. Shanghai: Sanlian shudian, 2008, 5:219. For a discussion of Xu Xu's early essays and fiction, see: Frederik H. Green. "The Making of a Chinese Romantic: Cosmopolitan Nationalism and Lyrical Exoticism in Xu Xu's Early Travel

Writings." *Modern Chinese Literature and Culture* (MCLC), volume 23.2, Fall 2011 (pp. 64–99).

3. According to Asabuki, Xu Xu asked her to replace his real name with the homophone *yu* 飫 in *The Other Side of Love* when they met in Tokyo after the war. Only in her later autobiography *My Paris Tales* from 1989 published after Xu Xu's death did she reveal his real name. See: Asabuki Tomiko. *Ai no mukō gawa* 愛のむこう側 [The other side of love]. Tokyo: Shinchōsha, 1977, 53–76. And: *Watakushi no Pari monogatari* 私の巴里物語 [My Paris tales]. Tokyo: Bunka shuppankyoku, 1989, 28–32.

4. For a summary and analysis of *Brothers* and other wartime works, see: Frederik H. Green. "Rescuing Love from the Nation: Love, Nation, and Self in Xu Xu's Alternative Wartime Fiction and Drama." *Frontiers of Literary Studies in China*, volume 8.1, Spring 2014 (pp. 126–53).

5. Shi Huaichi 石懷池. "Bangxian de mengyi 'Guilian'—Xu Xu de shu zhi yi" 幫閑的夢囈《鬼戀》—徐訏的書之一 [The trashy rigmarole "Ghost love": One of Xu Xu's books]. In *Shi Huaichi wenxue lunwenji* 石懷池文學論文集 [Collection of essays on literature by Shi Huaichi], edited by Jin Yi 靳以. Shanghai: Gengyun chubanshe, 1945, 151–54.

6. Xu Xu 徐訏. *Xu Xu wenji* 徐訏文集, 5:72.

7. Yan Jiayan 嚴家炎. *Zhongguo xiandai geliupai xiaoshuo xuan* 中國現代各流派小說選 [Anthology of works from the various modern Chinese literary groups]. Beijing: Beijing daxue chubanshe, 1986. See also his *Zhongguo xiandai xiaoshuo liupaishi* 中國現代小説流派史 [History of modern Chinese literary groups]. Beijing: Renmin wenxue chubanshe, 1989.

8. Xu Xu 徐訏. *Xu Xu wenji* 徐訏文集.

9. Wu Yiqin 吳義勤 and Wang Suxia 王素霞. *Wo xin panghuang: Xu Xu zhuan* 我心彷徨—徐訏傳 [My mind is restless: A biography of Xu Xu]. Shanghai: Shanghai sanlian shudian, 2008.

10. Green, Frederik Hermann. *A Chinese Romantic's Journey through Time and Space: Cosmopolitanism, Nationalism, and Nostalgia in the Work of Xu Xu (1908–1980)*. PhD dissertation, Yale University, 2009.

11. Christopher Rosenmeier. *On the Margins of Modernism: Xu Xu, Wuming-shi, and Popular Chinese Literature in the 1940s*. Edinburgh: Edinburgh University Press, 2017.

Note on the Translation

I have tried to stick as closely to the original Chinese text as possible. On a handful of occasions I have inserted an explanatory clause where there was none in the original. Words and phrases that are explained in the short prologue preceding each story are marked with an asterisk in the prologue and the translation.

Throughout the translation, I have maintained the Chinese convention of presenting the family name first and the given name last. All personal and place names are rendered in Hanyu Pinyin romanization, except for those names for which a standardized romanization other than Pinyin exists in English, as it does for some of the Taiwanese place names in "The All-Souls Tree." The one notable exception is in "When Ah Heung came to Gousing Road"; since the story takes place in Hong Kong, where Cantonese is predominantly spoken, all personal names are given in Cantonese romanization while all place names are reproduced according to the way they are customarily referred to in English in Hong Hong.

While many people have given me a helping hand with this translation, all mistakes are, of course, my responsibility.

BIRD TALK
and Other Stories
by Xu Xu

鬼戀
Ghost Love

The serialization of "Ghost Love" in January 1937 in the popular Shanghai bimonthly literary and current affairs journal *Celestial Winds* 宇宙風 made Xu Xu a literary celebrity in China. Xu Xu later considerably revised the original and published it as a book that, by 1949, had gone through nineteen printruns. "Ghost Love" evidently struck a nerve with the reading public of Republican-period China (1912–49). The translation presented here is based on the original from 1937.

The novel opens around the year 1930 when the first-person male narrator late one night meets a mysterious woman in front of a tobacco store on *Nanjing Road. Nanjing Road was the main shopping street in the International Settlement of Shanghai, the largely self-governed Anglo-American concessions area that had sprung up in Shanghai following the first Opium War of 1839–42 (see the map on pages 120–21). To the south, it bordered the French Concession, whose main thoroughfare was *Avenue Joffre, famous for its elegant shops, bars, restaurants, and theaters. Despite being a constant reminder of Western imperialism in China, the foreign concessions area emanated a cosmopolitan flair and came to symbolize urban modernity. Both the male narrator and the mysterious woman are thoroughly modern urbanites. She smokes *Pin Heads, a popular British cigarette brand, wears a *qipao, the tight-fitting dress that was popularized by Chinese socialites in Shanghai during the 1920s and 1930s, and speaks several foreign languages fluently. He wears an Omega watch, drinks brandy, and refuses to believe in ghosts, especially of the kind found in *Strange Tales from a Chinese Studio* 聊齋志異, a famous eighteenth-century collection of ghost stories.

The geography of Shanghai plays an important role in "Ghost Love," as it did in much of the fiction about Shanghai of the Republican period, in the same way the geography of Tokyo played an important role in modern Japanese fiction or that of New York, Paris, or Berlin in Western modernist fiction. The reader literally can follow the two protagonists on their nightly walk from the tobacconist on Nanjing Road to *Xietu Road 斜土路 on what would then have been the southern outskirts of Shanghai. On their nightly walk, they pass through *Xujiahui 徐家匯 (spelled Zikawei on old European maps), to the southwest of the French Concession. A Jesuit mission had existed there since the seventeenth century, on land that had been donated to the Catholic Church by the family of Xu Guangqi 徐光啓 (1562–1633), a prominent Jesuit convert. To this day, Xujiahui remains the site of St. Ignatius Cathedral. Completed in 1910, it was once the largest cathedral in East Asia (though it is now dwarfed by adjacent high rises). In its vicinity there were also Jesuit monasteries, schools, libraries, and an observatory.

Even further south and far beyond Xietu Road lies *Longhua 龍華, a district known to this day for its elaborate Buddhist temple and pagoda. In 1937, when the story was published, readers in addition would have associated Longhua with the location of a dreaded KMT prison. On April 12, 1927, Chiang Kai-shek betrayed his former Communist allies and ordered the violent purge of Chinese Communist Party (CCP) organizations in Shanghai. In the ensuing decade, until the fall of Shanghai to the Japanese in November 1937, thousands of political prisoners were held at Longhua Prison, many of whom were executed. After the founding of the People's Republic of China, the original site was turned into a martyr's shrine. The mysterious woman in the story appears to allude to the events of 1927 and, by claiming to work on behalf of the *masses, to the socialist cause that enjoyed broad support among progressive intellectuals in the 1920s and 1930s.

What I am about to relate happened six or seven years ago on a wintry evening around midnight. I was walking out of Xiangfen Alley and onto *Nanjing Road. The moment I turned the corner, right there by the tobacco store, I saw a woman entirely dressed in black. There was an incomparable pureness to her beauty and, strange as it might sound, I had the impression that somehow she looked familiar, yet I could not recall then where it was that I had seen her before. Was it because I was drawn to her beauty or because I wanted to figure out where I had seen her before? In any case, I could not help but throw another glance at her. I also no longer remember now whether that tobacco shop handed out matches or had an incense coil for their customers to light their cigarettes, but, just as she turned around, she let out a puff of smoke from the cigarette she was smoking and I got a whiff of its aroma. I am a bit of an expert when it comes to recognizing the smell of tobacco. Maybe it is a kind of talent: While studying at various universities in Europe, I attended lectures by maybe twenty professors, and I recognized them all by their tobacco. A hint of their tobacco, even with doors closed, was enough for me to tell who was standing in front of the door or walking past. Thus, the moment I smelled her cigarette, I knew she was smoking a *Pin Head. Surely Pin Heads were a little strong for that lady, and I immediately assumed that she must be a heavy smoker with blackened teeth. What a pity to have such exquisite beauty spoiled by a row of blackened teeth, I thought. I was already on my way again when she suddenly interrupted my thoughts:

"Human, tell me the direction to *Xietu Road!"

I jumped with bewilderment. As she spoke, I was able to see her teeth, or I should say: Her teeth grabbed my attention. They shone bright white, like a precious sword under the moon. But once she had closed her mouth again, I also noticed a particularly fierce look in her eyes. Her face, which at first had been lit up by the shop's red neon lights, was in fact silvery white and drained of all color. Her lips looked especially sallow and blood-less. Had she put on too much powder? Was she recovering from an illness? Still contemplating, I almost asked, Why don't you put on some rouge? But it was she who spoke again:

"Xietu Road, I said Xietu Road."

It suddenly occurred to me that the reason she looked so pale might be because her clothes were all black. She was wear-ing a black *qipao, black coat, black stockings, and black shoes. I also noticed that her clothes seemed much too thin. They were all single-layer, and the coat did not have a fur lining. Besides, her stockings were made of silk and she was wearing high heels. Could it be that her face was white from cold? I wanted to look at her fingernails, but she was wearing a pair of fine white gloves on her hands, one of which was holding the cigarette she was smoking.

"Human! Why are you looking at me like that?"

Her face was solemn, but overwhelmingly beautiful. It now made me think of the face of a silver female bust I had seen in a shop window somewhere along *Avenue Joffre in the French Concession of Shanghai. So that was why I had thought that I had seen her before! The beauty of her face lay in its harmo-nious structure that lacked any crudeness. I felt a little comical about my déjà vu experience, but nevertheless put on a serious face and said, "Even when asking for directions you should be a little polite. Fine if you don't want to call me 'Sir' or 'Master,' but how about a simple 'Mister'? What's this business calling me 'Human'? You are neither a goddess nor the almighty."

Actually, I was thinking that her beauty had something rather divine, and so my last sentence had been spoken some-what inadvertently.

"I am not a goddess," she replied. "I am a ghost."

Her face was of a chilling beauty, like that of a white jade that had been extracted from deep inside a mountain of ice. As for her voice, I can hardly find words to describe it. Were I to compare it to the sound of melting icicles hanging from a cliff in a tranquil valley and dripping drop by drop onto the surface of a perfectly still pond, then this might capture its clearness, but not its sharpness.

"A ghost?" I exclaimed laughing, and thinking to myself: "So one can see ghosts on Nanjing Road now."

"That's right, I am a ghost," she replied

"A female ghost walking the city streets, getting a light at a tobacco shop, smoking Pin Heads, and asking a gentleman for directions?" I had to laugh hard, supporting myself by leaning against a wall. It was cold and there was not a soul in the streets. I took out my pipe and started to smoke.

"You don't believe in ghosts?"

"Never believed in them until now, take my word for it. But if one day I do, it certainly won't be on Nanjing Road, and it certainly won't be on account of a beautiful woman who lights her Pin Heads at a tobacco shop and then asks some guy for directions."

"But surely you are afraid of ghosts?"

"How can I be afraid of them if I don't believe in them?"

"Well then, would you mind accompanying me to Xietu Road?"

"Why do you want to go there this late?"

"Because I know my way home from there."

"So how did you get here?"

"I walked and walked until I found myself in this place."

"I'll call you a cab to take you there."

"What's that supposed to mean? You can't walk that far? Or you think I can't call a cab myself?"

"So you are a ghost then, and you are not afraid of a stranger walking you to that godforsaken part of town?" I laughed again.

"Ghosts are at home in godforsaken places. It's you who should be afraid!"

"Afraid of what?"

"You ... you should at least be afraid of getting lost. You

know that ghosts plot their complex routes in deserted roads so that people unfamiliar with them will get lost? You must have heard the expression 'lost in the spirit world'? Well, in crowded places like Nanjing Road, it's ghosts who get lost because the routes of humans are even more complex."

"What you are saying is that you are a ghost who is 'lost in the human world' and it is for that reason that you can't find your way home anymore?"

"That's right."

"In that case, I'll accompany you, but you must then show me the way out from there."

"Of course."

For each of her last four replies she had worn a different facial expression, but taken together, all four formed yet another expression altogether. When she had uttered the first reply, she had raised her eyebrows. With the second, the corners of her eyes had trembled; with the third, her nostrils had flared up; and when she gave me her fourth reply, a dimple appeared on her cheeks and her white teeth sparkled. At that point, even if she had said that she would have to bite me to death once we had reached our destination, I still would not have declined her.

And so we started walking, as if we had given up waiting for the streetcar. She was smoking her cigarette and I was smoking my pipe. I was too absorbed by my own thoughts and hence was not talking, but soon she picked up the thread of our conversation.

"I guess you have never before walked the streets with a ghost, have you?"

"Neither am I now, and I don't foresee it ever happening."

"But you are walking with one by your side this very moment."

"I don't believe there are ghosts this beautiful."

"So you think a ghost ought to be less beautiful than a human?"

"That goes without saying. Humans turn into ghosts only after they die."

"You think that a ghost resembles a human corpse? Let me tell you, you are very much mistaken if you believe that the ugliness of a corpse in any way compares to the form of a ghost!"

She laughed out loud after she had said this. This was the first time I heard her laugh for, until now, she had only smiled silently. The sound of her laughter reverberated. When she stopped, it was as if the echo from her laughter slowly rose toward the sky, and even after it had already entered the clouds could still be faintly heard. I gazed at the sky.

"The ugliness of a corpse," she continued, "is the final destination of all human beauty, which is why there is no beauty in the human world. In the final analysis, all beauty is ugliness."

"But ghosts at best resemble humans and thus can never be more beautiful than they."

"You are not a ghost, so how do you know?"

"How about you, since you are not a human?"

"But I used to be a human, and a very lively one at that."

"And you still are now, I believe."

She gazed at the sky and said, "Nature for sure is beautiful."

"The night especially," I replied.

"Don't you think that the night is more beautiful than the day?"

"Yes, I think it is."

"And the night belongs to ghosts."

"If you really are a ghost, I admit that ghosts are a million times more beautiful than any human, but you are a human."

And so we kept walking. The conversation went from the beauty of ghosts to the existence of the soul, truth, and illusion, epistemology, ethics, and love. She cited the works of Plato and Aristotle, Kant and Fichte, Hegel, Schopenhauer, Nietzsche, and Bergson. She also talked about the Buddhist philosopher Nagarjuna and mentioned some other Indian names I do not remember, and she drew on Confucius and Laozi, Mencius and Zhuangzi, and even the idealist neo-Confucian Wang Yangming. She then talked about Freudian psychoanalysis and Einstein's theory of relativity, and even about electric waves and electrons.

At first, I was still trying to respond, but eventually all I did was listen to her. By then, we were already near *Xujiahui. It was deathly silent and freezing cold. Not a soul was in sight. The change in our surroundings added to my astonishment over her encyclopedic knowledge and slowly made me believe that maybe she really was a ghost after all. Yet I was not afraid, for there under the bright moonlight, my soul had already been completely captivated by her appearance and the way she carried herself. If she had wanted me to die, I would have obliged happily.

There was a gust of wind. I shivered and asked, "Aren't you cold?" I wanted to call her by her name, but suddenly realized that I did not know it. And so I added: "What should I call you?"

"You can call me Ghost."

"Ghost? I don't think I like that. Can't you tell me your name?"

"It's only because you are used to those common names typically given to humans, like Cuixiang, Baoying, Jumei, or Daiyu. That's why you also have to give a name to things non-human, just like when people call their dogs John or their cats Marie, or call a pavilion 'Drop of Verdant' and a mountain 'Heavenly Scale' or 'Celestial Eye.' It even goes as far as people calling their homes 'Villa Rustica,' 'Castle in the Clouds,' or 'Foggy Manor.' It's simply a sign of poor taste."

"Well then, how about I call you 'goddess'? Because if you really are not a human, then you surely must be a deity. And even if you turn out to be a human after all, the term 'goddess' still does justice to your noble bearing."

"I am a ghost all right, and there is no reason to believe that ghosts don't possess noblesse. What is it about the word 'ghost' that you find so deplorable? Since I am a ghost," she said angrily, "why do you want to call me 'goddess'?" But then she suddenly laughed and said, "Human, it turns out you are just an ordinary mortal."

She was of course right and so I kept silent. Our pace was slow, resembling more a leisurely stroll than a walk home. My eyes fixed on the horizon, I wondered whether she was observing me. I did not dare to meet her piercing gaze. The night was still and one could have heard the falling of a leaf. We walked in silence for about ten minutes until she said, "I think you should just call me 'ghost.'"

"But aren't there lots of ghosts? How could I be so generic and just call you 'ghost'?"

"Isn't it the same for humans? It would be just as generic as me calling you 'human.'"

"Exactly! But I leave it to you to call me whatever you wish to call me."

"I don't believe that humans are free to call each other whatever they like. In human society, isn't a son obliged to call a father 'father'? That's why one needs to follow a certain rationale when it comes to addressing humans."

"So what rationale does your method of address rely on?" I seemed to be losing ground.

"It's because you are the only human I know. If you don't know any other ghosts, either, then what's so irrational about calling me Ghost?"

"All right then, I won't argue anymore."

I seem to recall that afterward, we did not talk much until we got to Xietu Road. I wanted to see her all the way home, but she said it was at least another three miles and under no circumstances would she let me accompany her. We then agreed to meet again at a future date, at eight o'clock on a certain evening in the same place where we parted that night.

Our second encounter happened on a moonlit night. We wandered through some desolate parts of town, and by the time I returned home it was already dawn. The third time, we again met at the same place and again walked through extremely remote areas. I almost did not find my way home. From then on, our meetings became a routine, and we would meet once every three nights at the same place at the same time, rain or shine, and not once did either of us fail to show. She was a hearty walker and a great conversationalist. The reason I have little to show for in any one field of study, but instead like to read broadly, has much to do with her influence. She really was extremely erudite. Whether it was metaphysics or materialism, astronomy or entomology, she had something to say about everything. Once, we went to a café on Avenue Joffre that was run by a Jew. She spoke Hebrew to the owner and I guessed that she probably spoke quite a few other languages as well.

This friendship of ours had already lasted about a year and a half when one summer night while walking near *Longhua we got caught in a thunderstorm. Usually, when it looked as if it might rain, she would wear a raincoat and carry an umbrella, which she then would lend me in return for my hat. But that day, the rain had come unexpectedly. Since we were wearing summer clothes, we were drenched in no time. Had it been winter, I would have immediately wrapped my coat around her, but that day I was only wearing a thin cotton gown, which was soaked by the time the first two drops of rain had fallen.

"Human," she said, "today is your lucky day. I will grant you what you have begged me a hundred times and what I have always refused you. Come, let's go to my home to shelter from the rain."

And with that, she quickened her pace. The rain was so hard now I could barely keep my eyes open. Finally, we reached a village on the outskirts and after a couple more turns found ourselves in front of a door. She opened it with a key and pulled me in. We passed through a long dark corridor to reach a staircase. At the top of the stairs, there was a large, sparsely furnished room. It was decorated in an odd-looking way. All the furniture was made of mahogany. The bed was huge and had a black canopy the likes of which I had never seen still being used by people. But I had to content myself with admiring it from afar, for it stood at quite a distance from where she invited me to sit down around a table by the window. We smoked. Outside the window, I saw a large field that was bordered by two rows of single-storied houses from which not a speck of light emanated.

"Those houses …?"

"That's where the ghosts of our family live."

"And you live here alone."

"That's right."

She then served me some coffee and we quietly looked at the moon rising in the sky. Suddenly I noticed a Chinese flute and a violin on a shelf. "Ghost," I said (I had long gotten used to this form of address and thought it natural and rather intimate), "you play a number of instruments."

"I play a little, but it's just to distract myself when I feel lonely or bored. I am certainly no musician nor keen to be on stage."

I asked her to play a tune to embellish this quiet moonlit night and, facing the window, she began to play the violin. I stood behind her and waited for her to finish. When she turned around, I put my hand on her shoulder and, without knowing what I was doing, said, "Ghost, I love you, do you know that?"

But she freed herself and picked up a cigarette and a box of matches from the table. Her face was expressionless. I did not dare to look at her and waited for her to say something. She took a drag and exhaled the smoke, but she only spoke after she had exhaled for a second time.

"You know that you are a human and I am a ghost."

"You really think that humans and ghosts need to keep their distance?"

"No, but ghosts are weary of all human ways, and love we consider an extremely childish and laughable matter."

With the coming of dawn, she asked me to leave. She asked me to come back to this place after three days. She walked me to the door and pointed me in the direction home. After walking no more than a few steps, I looked back and saw that she had already returned inside. I walked back again and took out a red pencil (that was all I had on me) to leave a mark on the wall of her house. I wrote the words "mysterious existence." On the way back, I also made sure to remember every turn I took. I did not feel like going home to sleep and just wandered around until daybreak, when I went into a little teahouse. Over some tea and sesame cake, I contemplated that if she really were a ghost, then that house of hers should be a grave during the day, just as in all those old Chinese stories. I then took a nap in the teahouse until the sun had risen high in the sky, drank a couple of cups of warm wine, and, relying on my mental map, began to trace my steps back to her place. All along, my heart was beating fast with excitement. There really were only two possible outcomes: Either that house of hers was in fact a house, which would mean that she was a human, or else it was a tomb, which would mean that she really was a ghost. I was sure that I would soon have an answer.

Seen from afar, those rows of houses certainly did not resemble tombs. Could it be that they would turn into tombs once I approached? My eyes remained fixed on them.

Evidently, they were not tombs. My red markings were still there, which proved that I had come to the right place. So she had to be a human. Still, I wanted to get to the bottom of the matter and I thought up a plan: I would drop my pipe near the front door and then knock. When she asked me why I had come back, I would say that I was looking for my pipe. I would search for it in vain, but when she walked me out again, I would simply say, "Turns out I dropped it by the entrance!"

I knocked on the door for what seemed forever until finally someone opened it. It was an older woman who must have been in her sixties. She was hard of hearing.

"Excuse me, madam, I am looking for a young lady."

"Who are you looking for, mister?"

"I am looking for someone who lives here."

"No one else lives here. I have lived here for over forty years, but I have never seen you before."

"I want to visit a relative of yours, that lady who lives in the east-facing room upstairs. She usually wears black."

"Mister, I am hard of hearing. Please keep it short and tell me what it is that you want."

"Her last name is … Ghost. Actually … she's called …" As a matter of fact, I never did find out her name.

"What? Her last name is 'Ghost'? I have never heard of a last name 'Ghost.' Could it be that you have seen a ghost?"

"Madam, I am absolutely certain. You have to …"

"Mister, haven't I told you that I have lived here for forty years? No one else lives here." She was about to close the door on me, but I had already squeezed my foot and half of my body inside the entrance.

"Why don't you go some other place and ask. Don't waste people's time!"

"Madam, I am not kidding you. She really lives here. I came here only yesterday evening!"

"You must be crazy! You say you are here to see a young lady and that you came last night? If there really was a young lady living here, you certainly would not have been allowed to visit her at night. And why have you come back if you were here only yesterday?"

"I forgot something."

"What did you forget"?

"My pipe."

"Your pipe? Is it the one lying right there by the entrance?"

That old lady might have been hard of hearing, but her eyes were sharp. She pointed at the pipe on the floor and, quite obviously debunking my lie, said, "I say, mister, you are too muddle-headed. You dropped your pipe on the road in front of my entrance door. What made you say that you dropped it in the room of a young lady? Count yourself lucky that you ran into me. What you say is so preposterous, if it had been any-one else but me, you would have been slapped in the face, and rightly so."

What could I have said? Disheartened, I withdrew my foot and the door slammed shut. All I could do was pick up my pipe and reluctantly return home.

And so it was not until the evening of the third day that I knocked on that door again. I feared that my knocking would go unanswered, but to my surprise, Ghost immediately opened. That evening, we walked on the lawn inside the courtyard of her house and I told her about the story with the pipe.

"Human," she said calmly," I am invisible to you during the day, or do you still not believe I am a ghost?"

That day, when I was about to leave, I secretly placed my Omega wristwatch next to her violin. After I left, I went back to that same teahouse to take a nap. Then, after drinking a few cups of warm wine, I returned once more to her place and knocked on her door. After a long time, someone opened it. It was a servant who must have been in his fifties.

"I'd like to see your master," I said.

"My master? And what have you come to see my master about?"

"Your master and I are old friends." I assumed that she was the master of this house.

"Then how come I have never seen you?"

"Would you please be so kind and announce my arrival?"

He went inside and came back with an elderly gentleman who must have been past sixty.

Looking at me, the old gentleman asked his servant, "Who has he come to see?"

"He says he is an old friend of yours."

"An old friend of mine? Mister, who exactly are you looking for?"

"I am looking for a young lady who lives here."

"A young lady? No young lady lives here."

"I am not kidding you, sir, she is a friend of mine. She told me that she lives upstairs in the east-facing room. I have actually been to her room, and I recall that I left my wristwatch next to her violin."

"Let me assure you that no young lady lives here."

"So what is that upstairs room used for?"

"It's empty."

"Sir, please tell me. I am not a bad person. I am a friend of the young lady who lives in that room."

"That room really is empty. A young lady used to live there, but she died several years ago."

"How did she die?"

"Tuberculosis. She died before we even could take her to the hospital. We now keep that room empty, to commemorate her."

"And yet I assure you that I only recently have seen her. She likes to wear black clothes and smoke Pin Head brand cigarettes, doesn't she?"

"That's right, but it's what she used to like when she was still alive."

"Sir, that room of hers, can I take a look at it?"

"You want to take a look?"

"Yes. I am a friend of hers. I have been inside her room before. It's a single big room, isn't it? All the furniture is made of mahogany. There is a black canopy bed and there is a flute on a shelf and a violin, isn't that right?"

"That's all correct, only the canopy is white."

"White?"

"After she died, we were afraid that the canopy would get dirty and so we covered it with a black cloth. You see, you cannot have come here while she was still alive."

"Sir, there is no need to be suspicious of me. I am her friend, that's the truth, whether before she died or after. All I am asking is that you permit me to take a look at that room."

Part Two

He finally granted me my request and we went upstairs. He opened the door and we entered. It was dark inside. The room really looked as if no one had lived there in ages. For a long time, I held on to the chair where I had sat the previous night and so many other nights. I touched the objects I had used before with growing astonishment. Suddenly, my gaze met the mahogany bookshelf, and I exclaimed to the old gentleman with great excitement, "Will you believe me? There is a watch by the side of that violin and it's mine. It even has my name engraved on the back. Besides, it's still running."

The old gentleman, however, replied calmly, "That is impossible, mister."

I showed him my bare wrist, and extended my hand onto the shelf, but there was no watch. I felt around for it, but then withdrew my hand in frustration. The old gentleman did not seem surprised by this, and patting my back said, "Calm down. Even if you had put a watch here, it would have been such a long time ago that it would have stopped working by now and gone rusty. A person like her can die just like that, and you think your watch would not stop?"

"Sir, may I ask you in what relationship you stood to her?"

"She was like a daughter to me. We've done everything you asked, you have even seen her room, let's go back downstairs."

He walked me down and saw me to the door. Not another word was exchanged between us. Disappointed, I returned home.

On the night of our next rendezvous, just as I was about to take my leave, she returned my watch to me and said, "Last time, you forgot this. I wound it up for you, it's still running!"

This friendship of ours lasted for another year.

"You have lost weight," my friends said to me.

"You have grown haggard," my relatives noticed.

"How come you have changed so much?" the elders in my hometown remarked.

I had to think of the famous stories from *Strange Tales from a Chinese Studio,* in which people become possessed by ghosts, but I was not possessed by her. In fact, I still had my doubts as to whether she really was a ghost. I myself was convinced that the reason I looked haggard and worn was because of my staying up all night. My habit of reading and writing until the early hours started at that time.

Still, it would not have occurred to me to end our meetings on account of me being too tired. But nevertheless, one time I said to her: "Ghost (by now, calling her by that name felt just as intimate and normal as calling her 'darling'), could we not change the time of our meetings to daytime?"

"Daytime? You think a ghost can associate with a human during daytime? If coming here regularly in the middle of the night is too tiring for you, then how about coming only once every fortnight or once every month, or you can come once every two months."

"But you know that I love you."

"You are saying those words again, but those words only belong to the human realm. If humans could be in love with ghosts, then they also could be in love with cats or dogs."

"But it happens, it actually happens often in the human realm. Think of Duke Ling of Wei of the Spring and Autumn Period who loved his crane as much as he loved his concubine."

"But that was an unconscious emotion that belonged to the purely spiritual level."

"Does that mean that our love, too, belongs to …"

"On the spiritual level, I love you too. But since this love is only platonic, what's the use of dwelling on it?"

"Oh please! That man who loved his crane drove it around town in his chariot as if it were a concubine."

"You should remember that you are the only human who can come and go to my place as he pleases."

"But …" As I was saying this, I lowered my head toward hers.

She was seated, but clearly tried to evade me and said, "This isn't really a beautiful gesture to express your love. You see …" She took out a pencil and paper and drew a picture of two cows and two ducks kissing each other. "Or do you think this is beautiful?"

I laughed and said, "But you should know that in this mortal world, not everything needs to be beautiful. Besides, there is no one whom I adore more than you. That's why, if it does not cause you any physical or spiritual pain, I hope you will marry me."

"You must be kidding!" It was not meant to be funny, but she laughed anyway. And so, the night passed like all the others.

* * *

Quite some time had passed when, early one morning, some friends and I were visiting Longhua Temple. Suddenly, one of my friends exclaimed:

"Have a look at this nun here. What a stunning beauty!"

A nun came walking up behind us. Everyone seemed to pay her attention now, except me. I was racking my brains to think of an excuse for not having to accompany them back to Shanghai. Instead, I wanted to take the opportunity to pay a visit to Ghost. The nun was almost level with us now. My friends were staring at her in amazement. I followed their stare and was taken aback: Wasn't that Ghost? I tried my best to remain calm and turned my face so that she would not see me. Only when she had walked past did I turn around again. Everybody was marveling at her beauty.

I was no longer able to suppress my emotions and said to my friends, "Unfortunately, I did not get a glimpse of her face. I'll try to catch up with her to see where her convent is located. Maybe we can visit it some time."

Everyone thought this was a great idea, and so off I went.

"Don't wait for me," I told them as I left. "She might live far away."

I then followed her home, all the while keeping a distance of a few yards between me and her. Just as she was about to enter, I caught up with her and forced myself inside, exclaiming, "Walking the streets in broad daylight, are we?"

She was startled, but immediately composed herself and assumed that solemn expression of hers. She unhurriedly climbed the stairs and I followed her upstairs. She took off her hat under which she was wearing a tight headband. She disappeared into an inner room and came out again after having changed her clothes. Then she slowly asked, "When did you start following me?"

"Did you not see me amidst that group of friends?"

"Ghosts pay no attention to human affairs," she replied with deliberation, her eyes fixed to the floor.

"Today you have to admit that you are a human."

"But I really am a ghost!" She raised her head. Her expression was sincere, so absolutely sincere that it should have succeeded in whitewashing any lie, but this lie was simply too big.

Even though I was still not entirely free of doubt I said, "I can no longer believe that lie of yours. You are a human! At first you did not want me to know where you lived and made me believe that your home was a grave. After I had found your home, you created more illusions with the help of some other people. Then you said that you cannot enter the human realm during daytime, but today, you have to admit that you are a human. At least admit that you have been deceiving me!"

I was really agitated now, and I spoke with a loud and irritated voice.

She leaned against the back of the chair and began to cry. Finally she said, "Why can't you just let me be? Why do you have to insist that I am a human and drag me out of my grave and into this world? Why do you want me to live as a mortal in this monstrous world?"

This was the first time I had seen her cry, the first time I heard her speak in this tone of voice, part sad, part angry. I was moved, and kneeling down in front of her said, "Because I am a mortal, and I love you."

"But I don't want to be a human!"

"Now is no longer the time to talk like this. Please stop crying, and tell me why it is that you want to leave this world and live as a ghost."

"I don't want to recall, and I don't want to talk about it. Please leave, and don't come back again to disturb me. This is my world, my solitary world." Any trace of sadness had already vanished from her speech.

"But I love you. In this human world, I have been loved by many women, but I haven't loved any of them. But now you, who are not of this world, have driven me crazy." My voice was trembling a little because my heart was pounding.

She suddenly regained her composure. Her anger had completely subsided. She smiled a little, but her smile was colder than ice. Gracefully like a cloud, she moved over to the table, took a cigarette, and also handed one to me.

"Human, have a cigarette. Calm down, and get a grip on yourself." As she lit my cigarette for me she spat a mouthful of smoke into my face. Then she abruptly walked over to the window. I noticed that thick cloth curtains were drawn over all the windows, except for the two nearest to us. She held her cigarette in her mouth, and I saw the smoke escape through the open window, like a soul rising to the sky. She then let the curtain fall, first over the window where she was standing and then over the other one, before slowly sitting down on the sofa. A lamp with an amber-colored shade stood behind the sofa. She switched it on with the turn of her hand and said, "Even if I am a human being, believe me that I can instantly turn into the kind of ghost you might imagine."

I saw that she was holding a shiny little dagger. I had often seen that dagger and even tinkered with it, but in the past, I had only thought of it as a trinket. Now I realized that it also was a lethal weapon.

"If circumstances or the will of others won't permit me any longer to live like a ghost, then this dagger can turn me into a real ghost at once. It's not much that separates a human from becoming a ghost."

She had spoken these words in a cold and sharp voice. The amber light of the lamp shone on her face, her hand, and the dagger she was still holding. Her gaze was piercing. All this gave the scene a threatening atmosphere. Unwittingly, I dropped the cigarette I was still holding between my lips. I was losing my wits. In a flash, I sensed all the witchcraft of a sorceress and the art of a hypnotist. I turned my eyes away from hers and stared at her feet. I was completely under her spell. My gaze still fixed at her feet, I thought, "Maybe she really is a ghost? But even if she is a human, she surely possesses some magic."

It took me about a minute to regain my senses, and for my brain to work rationally again.

"Let's pretend it's night," she suddenly said calmly. "You sit over there. Let your mind be as placid as the light that surrounds us, and let us talk about events far removed from this world."

"So tell me first, why is it that you want to leave the human world and live in this way? Why is it that you want to be a ghost when quite clearly you are a human? And why won't you allow me to love you?"

I had gotten up to seize the dagger from her. I was watching her attentively, but she avoided my gaze. She had lowered her head and her hair covered her face. No one spoke for the duration it takes to smoke half a cigarette. I sat down in an arm-chair in front of her. With my elbows resting on my knees I leaned forward toward her, my eyes still focused on her. The distance that separated us was no more than two feet. I was waiting for her reply, fiddling all the while with the dagger that measured about ten inches.

"Of course I also used to be a human in the past," she finally said. "In fact, I gave my all to humanity. What's more, I was in love with someone who cared infinitely more about humanity than you."

"And ...?"

"We were engaged in revolutionary activities. We worked in secret, enduring countless hardships and traveling many roads." Her tone of voice was gloomy at first, but then all of a sudden was filled with vigor.

"Human, tell me, what exactly is it that you love in me?"

"Love is intuitive," I replied. "I simply love you, without rhyme or reason. I venerate the beauty I see in you."

"So you see some kind of beauty in me, but have you ever calmly analyzed your feelings? Where exactly lies my beauty?"

"I feel that you possess an otherworldly beauty. There is nothing ordinary about you. When you move, you have the nimbleness and grace of an immortal, and when you are still, you have the solemnness of a Buddha."

"If what you say is true, I was only able to attain this otherworldliness by enduring the cruelest of worldly struggles."

I did not understand what she meant.

"I attempted as many as eighteen assassinations. Thirteen times I was successful, five times I wasn't. I escaped a hail of bullets, fled by steamship, crossed the desert, and slipped away through busy city streets. I broke out of jails. Do you believe me? It's through these kind of struggles that I have obtained the air of an immortal."

She smiled derisively.

"And during life in jail, sitting quietly in the damp darkness of my prison cell with eyes closed, day after day, month after month, I assumed the solemnness of a Buddha, if you believe it."

She changed her tone.

"Maybe you don't believe me. You don't believe I am a ghost, and you believe even less that I have killed people. With that little dagger alone, I have killed three men and one woman."

After a frightening pause, she continued.

"Later, for several years, I went into exile abroad, wandered about, studied. Only after I came back did I learn that the man who had fought by my side and whom I had loved had been arrested and executed. I drowned my sorrow by immersing myself in political work and I offered my love to the *masses."

She again changed the tone of her voice.

"But later, there was defeat after defeat. Some betrayed their friends, others sold secrets, some joined the ranks of officials, some got arrested, some died. Of that band of comrades, only I remained, resigning myself to this bitter solitude. I have seen this world, I have tasted life, and I have probed into the depth of the human heart. I want to be a ghost, yes, a ghost." She got up, aroused by her own words, but then sat down again and continued, haltingly.

"But I don't want to die. Only nothingness awaits the dead. I still want to observe the vicissitudes of this world. That's why I choose to live as a ghost."

"And the people downstairs are your parents?"

"No." Again she changed her tone of voice. "You think I am Chinese? No, human, I am Jewish. My mother was Jewish and my father was an overseas Chinese. Neither of them has ever been to China. But they are both dead now. This is the home of the man I used to love. His parents moved here for their son. They mourn their son, and they pity me. That is why I was able to come and live here like their daughter. They even respect my wish and treat me as if I were a ghost. It's been like this for so long now that they have gotten used to it. It's just like they said: This room is kept in memory of their deceased daughter."

She continued: "I have been living here for several years now. At first, I never went out, and passed the days reading. Later, I started to go for walks at night and, later still, I went out in daytime, dressed as a nun and taunting this world."

I cannot recall now the surge of emotions I experienced while listening to her, but when I had heard her out to the end, it was as if I had been instantly cured from insanity. I felt as if I had walked out of a maze in which I had been trapped for several years or as if a tumor that had grown bigger year after year in my heart had all at once been cut out. There was brightness before my eyes and my entire body felt invigorated.

She suddenly got up and said, "Human, now I have told you everything. I want to live alone in this world and I hope that from now on you won't disturb me anymore. I don't want you to come here again." As she was speaking, she drew away from me.

I moved closer to her and said, "But I love you, and that is the truth. I heard everything you said, and it has left me more elated than bewildered. It's just as if you resolved for me a theoretical problem I had long been unable to solve. I feel light-hearted and dazzled by love that shines bright because you are my source of light. I don't want to call you Ghost anymore, I want you to be a human being, and I want to be the human at your side."

"You want me to be a human being? What kind of human being? I have already been every kind," she replied in a chilling tone.

But I felt my heart go on fire, because it had been rid of a demon. My whole body glowing, I exclaimed, beside myself with joy, "I want you to be a human being capable of rejoicing in life! I want you to be happy, to enjoy. In this world, you have already sacrificed enough of your blood and tears for the good of society. From now on, you must rejoice in life! I know that you love me. Listen to me: Love, and seize the day!"

There was a bottle of brandy on the shelf. I poured two cups, gave one to her, and said, "To love! Let's finish this glass. I cherish this chapter in our lives and this love of ours. Let us strive to fill the next chapter with happiness."

By the time she had finished her cup, my lips were already over hers. I felt energized and courageous like never before. Even today, I can still feel that kiss on my lips. It was to be the only one.

"Tell me that you love me," I said to her.

"I suppose I love you. Otherwise I would not have permitted you to enter into my world. But now please leave, my mind needs some rest."

"But where do we go from here?"

"From here? Come back tomorrow evening. Let me regain my energy first before I talk to you again."

I saw her lie down on her bed and left.

* * *

I do not know how I managed to pass that night and the following day. Neither my heart nor my limbs nor the cells in my body could find rest for one minute. I fantasized about what lay ahead and made plans for the future. I imagined how it would be to live under one roof and to go traveling together. I thought about our life side by side, and about what it would be like many years from now. Once dusk had fallen the following day I set out to her place. Along the way, I tried to guess her mood and her dress and the tone of voice in which she would talk to me. My heart had grown wings, it seemed, and constantly wanted to fly off to her. I finally arrived at her door.

To my utter surprise, it was an old lady who opened the door. Paying her no attention I was about to storm in, but she addressed me.

"Mister, the young lady has left this morning for a long journey."

"Who has left?"

"That young lady. She left behind a letter for you."

My heart was beating hard. I tore open the letter, but since it was already dark, I was not able to make out the words. Only after I had taken out my lighter was I able to read the letter clearly:

Human: The time we spent together was nothing but a dream. That dream cannot—and should not—become reality. I am going on a far-away journey so that I can escape from reality. When I am no longer coerced by reality, I might return. But it might be three or four years until then. From now on, I will continue to live the life of a ghost. I hope you will live the life of a human, and do so decently.

I almost fainted. I walked out in silence, feeling dejected and depressed. My heart was heavy with grief and my body no longer supported the weight of my soul. I do not know for how far I walked until I passed out along the road.

I must have gotten lost. I found myself amidst small street stalls, but all was quiet and deserted. Occasionally, someone would pass in the distance, only dimly discernible. I was exhausted. I knew I was in the realm of ghosts and, no matter how hard I tried, I could not find a way out. Besides, no one paid any attention to me.

Just when I wanted to sit down in a corner to take a rest, I suddenly caught sight of her and exclaimed, "So this is where you are!"

"I told you that I am a ghost," she replied.

"Well …"

"None of these roads lead to the human world, they only lead to heaven." Without uttering a word, she pulled me by the hand and, just as if we were walking on flat ground, we walked toward the sky. Suddenly, I felt cold and wet, and my breathing became heavy. I noticed that she was wearing clothes that appeared to be made of black gauze.

"Aren't you cold?" I asked her.

She smiled and said, "No, not me, but I know that you are cold, because the dew is falling. It means we have arrived in the human world."

When I awoke, I was confused. I was lying by the roadside, enshrouded in dew. I could hardly remember anything. I could not tell apart my life of the past two or three years from the dream I had just woken from. I tried to pull myself together. It was autumn and already quite chilly. Like in a trance, I dragged myself on, leaning against a lamppost every few yards. I did not know what time it was. Was it still night or already morning? I was no longer conscious of anything. I remember that dawn had already broken when I finally reached Shanghai and found a cab. I do not remember anything of the journey home. When I arrived, I did not say a word, but I could feel that I was sick. My family went to call for a doctor. Soon after, I was admitted to a hospital.

Everyone asked what had happened to me, but I did not tell them anything. My sickness tied me to my bed for two months, but when I was finally able to get up, I went straight to Ghost's house. All along, I had harbored a lingering suspicion that maybe the events of the past two or three years had all been a dream. But everything was just as I had remembered. It was the old lady who answered the door. No, the young lady had not returned, she informed me. After two months I went back again, but she still had not come back. After four months, I once more went to see her, but there was still no sign of her. Another three months went by, and she still had not come back.

The last time I went was two years ago during winter. It was snowing lightly when I reached her house. I almost did not recognize the door, because it had been newly painted in red. The person opening the door was a middle-aged farmer, which only added to my surprise.

He did not know anything. Only when I asked about the old couple and the young lady did he finally exclaim, "Oh, that old couple passed away one after the other. After the young lady buried the old lady, she sold the house and everything in it. She only took four cases of books with her when she left."

"So ..."

"The new owner is named Wang. I am his servant."

"Would you mind notifying your master that I would like to meet with him? You can tell him that I am a relative of the previous owner."

Not long after he had gone back in did Mr. Wang emerge. He was also an older man, and he repeated what his servant had already told me. He then invited me in to sit down, and I said to him, "Mr. Wang, I only want to find out what happened to the young lady. I am a relative of hers. When the house was sold, were you personally in touch with her?"

"Yes, someone introduced us, and later she dealt with me directly."

"Do you remember what clothes she was wearing?"

"Ah yes, that was a little strange. She always wore black."

"And wasn't she smoking Pin Head brand cigarettes?"

"She was smoking, but I am not sure if it was Pin Heads."

"And she also sold all the furniture in the house to you?"

"Yes, but why are you asking me all this?"

"To tell you the truth, I am very familiar with this place, which is why I care so much. The east-facing upstairs room, doesn't it have eight windows? And don't the windows all have thick cloth curtains? And on one side of the room, isn't there a mahogany-colored bed? And on the other side, there is a sofa and two chairs with purple covers, no?"

"That was the young lady's room. How come you ...?"

"We are close relatives. I was raised here from a young age.

Later I left for several years, but after I came back to Shanghai, I came here frequently. I was the one who arranged the furniture. I have just returned to Shanghai and had planned to stay here. I didn't expect that my uncle and aunt had passed away. That's why I would like to find out the whereabouts of the young lady. Mr. Wang, do you know where she went?"

"That I really don't know, but if you ..."

"Mr. Wang, may I ask what you are using that room for now?"

"Right now it's empty. My son is away on account of his work. He will come back next year to get married. The room will be the bridal chamber for the newlyweds."

"The furniture in that room hasn't been moved, has it?"

"That's right, mister. It won't be until next year that I might rearrange it."

"Mr. Wang, I have an exceptional request. As a matter of fact, I am very attached to this house. What's more, when my uncle was still alive, he had actually suggested that the room should be my bridal chamber after I get married. That's why I implore you to allow me to rent the room for a year and to live there until fall next year. I will of course move out should you be in need of the room."

"But ..."

"As far as you are concerned, Mr. Wang, the room is empty anyway. I will live here by myself and won't bother you too much. If you don't believe me, I can give you a deposit."

"So just yourself?"

"Yes, there won't be anyone else. It's just because I have a special attachment to this house. This house now belongs to you, and I just would like to live here for a while, just like someone visiting an old friend."

He finally agreed, and for a monthly rent of twenty yuan, I lived there from winter that year until last fall. I did not move any furniture. Every day, I imagined what her life had been like while she had lived there and I tried to relive it. I evoked the past, fantasized about the future, and dreamt I do not know how many dreams. The year passed quickly, and when fall came, I got ready to move out. Mr. Wang invited me to stay for his son's wedding banquet, but I was too overcome by grief. Leaving a monetary gift for the newlyweds, I took my leave.

I have stayed in Shanghai since winter last year. I cannot help it, but every other day, I will head to the tobacco shop on the corner of Xiangfen Alley and Nanjing Road. I will then invariably end up wandering all by myself to Xietu Road and then on to Longhua, smoking Pin Heads along the way. Only when dawn approaches will I head home. Until now, I have not found the courage to pay a visit to the Wangs and the house where I lived for a year. It is summer now, and I remember clearly what happened last summer. I also remember clearly what happened the summer two years ago, and the summer before that. Summer has come back again, but what once happened will never repeat itself. I miss her terribly, and there is not a moment when I am not thinking of her. Where in this wide human world will I ever see her again?

June 11, 1936 (revised on July 11)

猶太的彗星
The Jewish Comet

Xu Xu wrote this short story in May 1937 in Paris, where he had arrived a few months earlier to pursue studies in philosophy and psychology. Like several other stories he wrote during this time, it describes a romance between a cosmopolitan Chinese first-person male narrator and an exotic woman, in this case of Jewish heritage. In hindsight, the story might appear to trivialize the tragedy of the Jewish people in Europe that was unfolding. However, the story bespeaks the genuine interest cosmopolitan readers in Shanghai took in East-West encounters and in European politics. Popular current affairs journals such as *Cosmic Winds* 宇宙風 or *Western Wind* 西風 not only published many of Xu Xu's exotic romances in those years but also frequently discussed the civil war in Spain and the growing anti-Semitism in Germany, both topics "The Jewish Comet" engages with.

The choice of a Jewish protagonist further illustrates just how much the Jewish struggle featured in the imagination of Chinese intellectuals since at least the end of the Qing dynasty. Not only did it allow for ready identification with tales of national suffering, it also bore the potential to heighten Chinese readers' own sense of nationalism and national survival. Similarly, the female protagonist's association with the Spanish Civil War is not bereft of historical likelihood. A considerable portion of the volunteers fighting in the International Brigade were, in fact, Jews. Another important plot detail appears to be based on historical fact: Fascist Italy was an important supplier of manpower, war machinery, and ammunition to Franco's forces in Spain.

Jews also formed a sizable contingent of foreigners living in Shanghai, some of whom were Baghdadi Jews who had come with the British following the Opium Wars; others were Russian Jews who had fled their homeland and the subsequent civil war following the October Revolution. In the wake of Hitler's rise in Germany and the ensuing systematic persecution of Jews in Germany and the territories that eventually fell under German control, Shanghai saw a further influx of some 18,000 Jewish refugees, most of whom arrived between the fall of 1938 and the summer of 1939. The narrator in the short story sails to Europe aboard an Italian steamer, presumably of the Lloyd Triestino line, whose flagship *Conte Verde* Xu Xu had taken on his passage to Europe the previous year. Incidentally, the *Conte Verde* and her sister ship *Conte Rosso* played a crucial role in helping many of the desperate European Jewish refugees reach Shanghai.

Like "Ghost Love," "The Jewish Comet" also reveals to the reader much of the reality of life in the Foreign Concessions in prewar Shanghai. Sherkels, the Jewish tailor in the story, has a store on *Avenue Joffre, the main thoroughfare of the French Concession known for its elegant boutiques as well as numerous bars and restaurants. Prior to the narrator's departure, Sherkels invites him to his apartment, which appears to be located in a modern tenement building of the kind built in Shanghai in the 1920s and 1930s to absorb the ever-growing population. The word *"apartment" appears in English in the original. Inside the foreign concessions, several *foreign-language newspapers circulated and a plethora of languages could be heard.

When I awoke, all I could see through the porthole was the open sea. I immediately thought of her. Had she gotten sick? Had this big plan been abandoned after all? Yet when I got out of my bunk to have a cigarette, I saw two unfamiliar pieces of luggage. When I also noticed some items of makeup and some toiletries next to the washbasin, I knew that she must have come on board after all. Still, I was not entirely sure yet, because when I had gone to bed, it was three in the morning. The ship had been scheduled to sail at four. Could she really have embarked that late? I wanted to find out and slipped into my shoes. The lower bunk was empty, but the blanket was tousled. She must have already gotten up. Yes, indeed, she must have already gotten up, because her toiletries were wet. In addition, I spotted two brown strands of hair in the washbasin. I could not remember whether her hair had been brown or black or blond, but these strands surely must have been hers. It was already ten. I hurriedly washed and went to the dining room to have breakfast. She probably had already finished hers and stepped out on deck, I thought. There were still a few scattered passengers in the dining room. Even before I could step inside and see if maybe she was still there, I noticed a woman dressed in blue and gray, waving at me from a table on the left. I had no idea whether it was her or not, but since it was a European-looking woman who was waving at me, it had to be her.

When I walked over to her, she took hold of my hand, giving the semblance of intimacy and familiarity. I sat down across from her. She asked me if I had slept well the previous night and what time I had boarded the ship, as well as a whole lot of other questions. I am usually not much of a conversationalist, and all I could do as she was quizzing me over breakfast was reply to her questions, even if I had wanted to ask something in return. Only when she had finished breakfast and taken out a cigarette did I finally have a chance. I took out a match and, lighting her cigarette for her, asked, "It must have been close to four when you came on board?"

"Yes," she said, hastily exhaling her first drag of smoke. "I thought it might bother you if I came on board any earlier. When someone from China sails to Europe, it's just like when we Europeans travel to China. It's such a long journey, and there surely were a lot of relatives and friends who came to see you off. Wouldn't it have raised eyebrows if they had seen you depart with a foreign woman?"

"Miss, but I thought ..."

"Now don't call me that, we are already husband and wife! Husband and wife should not address each other in that way, according to neither Chinese nor Western customs, isn't that right? You had best address me by my first name. I am called Catherine."

I blushed a little. I, a thirty-plus-year-old divorced father of a daughter and a son, made to blush by a twenty-something-year-old woman....

I began to have regrets, regretted that I had agreed to her becoming my wife. How had all this come about? It had begun three months earlier. After the Ministry of Education announced that it would send me to Europe to study vocational education, I made my way to Shanghai to prepare for my stay abroad. I had never had the habit of wearing Western-style clothes, and so I had to purchase an entire wardrobe, from necktie to dress shirt. I found a shop on *Avenue Joffre in the French Concession of Shanghai that was comparatively inexpensive. The store was tiny and its owner was accountant, sales clerk, and assistant all in one. My several purchases at the store had led me to become acquainted with the owner, who was named Sherkels. He told me that he was Norwegian and that he was Jewish. He was short and plump, had a mustache, and was in his forties. He told me that he had gotten around quite a bit and that he spoke several languages. My first destination was going to be France and, because my French was pretty rusty, I took the opportunity to practice with him whenever he was not too busy with his store. He usually wasn't. Business was slow, probably because it was the middle of summer. I would buy a few things, and then chat with him for an hour or two. He liked to talk, and he would often complain that times were bad and that the world was in a depression. No matter which industry or which country, things were tough, he would say. I also asked him a lot about life in Western Europe and about his personal experiences, and I naturally told him that I was going to travel to Europe.

One Sunday, I was going to meet a friend at a café. When I entered, I ran into Sherkels. He was on his own, reading a newspaper in a corner under an electric fan. A bottle of beer stood on the table in front of him, and when he saw me he called me over. I ordered an ice cream and sat down across from him.

"The weather is hot!" he groaned with a laugh.

"It sure is," I replied. "You are a big man, so it must be even hotter for you. Do you often come here?"

"Yes, I do. When I lived in France I acquired the habit of frequenting cafés."

"Do you always come on your own?"

"As soon as I get here, I always run into friends."

I was about to say that he probably had not expected to run into me when his eyes suddenly caught sight of someone behind me. I inadvertently also turned around and saw two women emerge from the back of the café. When I turned around again, I saw that he had gotten up and was waving at them in an extremely affectionate way. I looked again at the two women and noticed that they, too, were smiling and greeting him. Sherkels had already walked over and was talking to them. I felt awkward looking at them from where I sat and turned around again. I picked up Sherkels's newspaper, but I did not even notice whether it was a Russian, English, or Chinese *paper. Instead, I was wondering what connection Sherkels might have to those two women who most definitely were also regulars at this café. After a short while, he came back to his seat. I glanced at the two women as they left, and I thought that the one wearing a yellow dress was really quite pretty.

"Were those two Jewish girls?" I asked him. "They were beautiful!"

"You think so? I should have introduced them to you. Speaking about beauty, I think the Chinese are more beautiful than any other people."

And so we kept chatting. The friend I had been waiting for and looked forward to seeing never showed up and I forgot all about him. At some point, Sherkels suddenly said, "Let me invite you for a drink!" and he presently ordered a few snacks and some beer. By the time we finally parted around five in the afternoon, he treated me like an old friend and told me to meet him again at the café.

I did not return to that café. Still, since he had invited me despite us only being casually acquainted, I felt obliged and invited him to a Cantonese restaurant in return a few days later. He drank a lot that day and, with his tongue loosened, talked much about his past and about international affairs. He hated war and cursed the global arms race.

"During the Great War we fought battle after battle, but for what?" he exclaimed. "Was there any gain? And for what price? How many buildings were destroyed, how many people killed? I myself must have killed over a thousand people. Why do we have to kill people, even if we have no ill feelings toward them?" He was clearly getting very agitated.

"You took part in the war?" I asked.

"Who didn't? At that time, even sixteen-year-old boys had to take part! Of the four years of war, I spent three in the trenches and six months in a hospital. Tens of thousands of people went mad!"

"Then you were lucky that you did not die." I said.

"No, I did not die, but should I consider myself lucky? Who knows, I might well have to see another war. Besides, life has become dull and empty because of the experience of that long war. You think about it, all my old friends died. I saw them die one after the other, right next to me. They fell to the ground, and I never saw them rise up again. My family was wiped out by the war. My mother, wife, and daughter perished during the war. What is there left for me to live for? The father of one of the girls you saw the other day at the café, the one in the yellow dress, was a good friend of mine. We had been friends since childhood, but he died, without rhyme or reason. If he hadn't died, he'd surely be a great musician now. He was a musical genius, and he was diligent. Even in the trenches he did not give up his violin. What is there left to say? That genius was sacrificed for no reason, and he was not the only one. What were all those sacrifices for? And what about the man who killed him? He was just like me. Among those thousands that were killed by me, there surely must have been scientists and artists, maybe even a musician. I love music, and if that person had not been killed by me, he might have become my friend and a member of my cultural circle. Tell me, why did I have to commit these crimes? I don't believe I am free of sin. Even killing one person out of love is a sin, so how can killing thousands of people without rhyme or reason not be a sin? I used to be a devout believer, but when we were told that we were absolved of sin because what we did was for glory or for whatever, I lost all faith in religion."

He wanted to keep on drinking, but when I saw how agitated he had become, I urged him to stop. When we left, I called a car and took him home. Maybe it was because we had had some fruit for dessert that he was still quite clear-headed.

"I am not drunk," he said. "I am not drunk, but whenever I drink I get carried away.... I am sorry."

I went home and thought to myself that he was certainly not an ordinary merchant, but a delightful person with a conscience.

From then on, I went to see him at his shop whenever I had nothing to do. I sometimes would also take some friends or relatives who wanted to buy some items of clothing. One day, when I went to see him with a relative who wanted to buy a bathing suit, he exclaimed the moment we stepped into the store, "Mr. Xu, how come you haven't stopped by these past days? There is something I have to discuss with you."

"What's the matter?" I asked.

"Let's talk tomorrow. Why don't you come to my home tomorrow evening at seven to dine with me and my family?" He took out a name card.

"With your family at your home? Did you not say that your whole family had been killed during the war?" I asked, smiling awkwardly.

"Ah! This here is my new family, the one I established after I came to China," he said, pointing at the address on the name card.

To tell the truth, I accepted the card and his invitation because my curiosity had gotten the better of me. At the same time, I was also a little ill at ease. What was it that he wanted to discuss with me? I wanted to ask him, but just then some other customers entered the store, and we soon left. I could not guess what it was that he wanted to discuss with me and in the end I thought that maybe, after all, there was nothing in particular and he just wanted to invite me over as a friend.

The following day at six, I went to the address on the card. He lived in a right-facing *apartment on the third floor of a modern tenement building. I knocked on his door and he immediately opened it. There were two larger rooms that served as bedrooms and a smaller one that served as a dining and living room. Then there was the kitchen, which was even smaller, and next to the kitchen was the bathroom. He introduced me to his wife, who probably was close to forty and who must have been very beautiful when she was young. Her manner was gentle and her demeanor almost resembled that of a Chinese.

His wife went into the kitchen and the two of us chatted on the sofa in the living room. He did not raise the matter that he had wanted to discuss with me and instead engaged in small talk about the cost of rent in Shanghai and the like. After a while, I noticed two photographs on the wall. One of them seemed to be a family photograph with him standing in the middle and looking very young.

"Is that your family?" I asked.

"Yes," he said. "Those are my father and mother, my wife and my daughter."

"How about this one?" I pointed at the other one.

"Ah, that is me, can't you tell? And that is my friend, the musical genius, the father of the young lady you saw the other day." Seeing that I showed interest in his past, he reached for a big photo album from beneath the coffee table. Leafing through the pages, he explained to me who was in the photographs. There were quite a few of his friend, the musician, and of his friend's daughter from when she was a child. There was one for almost every year, starting from when she was an infant. In some, she could be seen with her mother, on others she was holding a doll or sitting next to her father at the piano, holding a violin. In others still, she could be seen with relatives and friends. These photographs aroused in me a deep-felt sympathy for her, a fatherless child, wandering in a foreign land. Only when his wife brought out dinner did he put away the album. During dinner, I casually chatted with his wife. He never once mentioned the matter that he had wanted to discuss.

After we had finished dinner and his wife had cleared the table, he invited me to sit on the sofa with him. Each of us holding a cup of coffee in our hands and a cigarette between our lips, he finally said, "Aren't you taking an Italian liner to sail to Europe?"

"Yes," I replied.

"Well, that's great. If you agree, she can go with you."

"Who?"

"The daughter of my friend."

"She wants to go to Europe?"

"Yes, her father's sister passed away and she is going back to claim an inheritance."

"I see. Why should we not be able to travel together?" I asked, but seemingly no longer paying attention to my words, he continued:

"Her aunt loved her very much. After both of her parents had died, she lived with her aunt. Later, when her aunt's husband passed away, her aunt remarried. Eventually, she came to China with her father's younger brother and his wife. The person whom she was at the café with the other day was her uncle's wife. She runs a flower shop here in Shanghai and my friend's daughter helps her out. When her aunt in Europe died, the testament stipulated that she should inherit half of all her aunt's personal effects, but only after she has gotten married. It has already been two years, but because she hasn't yet married, she hasn't gone back."

"So she should wait until she gets married," I said.

"But it's not easy to find the right person, given the circumstances," he said. "At the same time, she wants to claim the inheritance now. And that's what I wanted to discuss with you, because there isn't anyone more suited for this than you."

"I don't understand what you mean," I said.

"It's very easy: I am asking you to marry her in name only. Once she has claimed her inheritance, you can go your own way again."

"You do know that I was a married man and that I have children?" I replied.

"What's the problem? The whole thing is for show only. She will nominally use 'Mrs. Xu' in her passport and, once you get to Europe, all you will have to do is go to the attorney together. And that will be the end of it."

"I will have to think it over carefully," I said.

"Yes, go ahead and think it over, but please don't think that I have any ulterior motives. I am only helping her out because

her father was my friend. I know a lot of Westerners in Shanghai
who are always traveling to Europe, but none of them is a good
fit. Many of them would not be able to keep a secret. Others are
just crude traders or hoodlums who lack integrity and who cannot be trusted. There is no way of telling what they would …"

He fell silent and took a drag on his cigarette, but I knew
what he meant.

Was I thinking it over? As a matter of fact, I had already
made up my mind to help her. First, I pitied that young woman;
second, I wanted to satisfy my curiosity; and finally, I did believe
that Sherkels was not the kind of person who would set me up or
use me. After all, there were no ill feelings between us.

"I hope you will think it over and let me know," he said. "Oh
yes, and one more thing: Your steamer ticket. You can purchase
it with her, or ask her to purchase it for you, because a relative of
her uncle's wife works for the shipping company and can get a
forty percent discount."

After he had said this, he probably feared that I would get
suspicious and hastily said, "It's not about the money, but you
can get a better cabin, and have it a little nicer. Also, you don't
speak Italian and you don't know your way around Italy. She can
take you places."

It is possible that I was somewhat swayed by the prospect
of a discounted steamer ticket, but truth is that I really wanted
to get to know that young lady, and so I said, "If all I need to do
is really as simple as you say it is, then I am happy to do it. But I
am traveling third class."

"Right, third class," he said while shaking my hand. "She
is also taking third class. It's silly to take second class anyway,
because the cabins and amenities are more or less the same." He
then asked me for my address and phone number. At that time,
I was staying in the house of my relatives, and I wrote down the
address for him.

"Once the ticket is issued," he said, "I will let you know and
we can go and pick it up together."

Shortly after, I briefly returned home to see my family in the countryside. On the first day after my return to Shanghai, I learned that Sherkels had already called. I rushed over to see him, and together we went straight to the offices of the shipping company. My ticket had already been issued, and I paid the discounted price.

When we left, Sherkels asked me, "Would you like to go on board and see your cabin?" Naturally I wanted to see it, and so the two of us got on a tram to the docks.

Number sixty-one was a double cabin. It had an upper bunk and a lower bunk, and it had plenty of natural light. My ticket was for the B bunk, which was the upper bunk.

"A double cabin?" I asked.

"Exactly! Next door is a cabin for four!" He seemed to imply that a double cabin was of course far superior to a cabin for four.

"So, the lower bunk is ..."

"The lower bunk is hers."

"Why did she have to get one in the same cabin?" I asked. What I meant was that although I was her cover so that she could claim her inheritance, there was no need for us to share a cabin on the steamer.

"Oh, she was the one who ordered the tickets," he said, "and since no special requests had been made, I guess the company must have assumed you were husband and wife, and a double cabin naturally is a far better cabin." He seemed not to find anything remotely strange about it. I, however, felt uneasy, and it must have shown on my face.

"It shouldn't bother you," he said, smilingly. "You are too ... And anyway, you are a married man."

"It doesn't bother me, it's just a little inconvenient," I said with a forced smile.

"If it's a problem, I will ask her to board late, so that your wife won't see her."

"I don't have a wife," I said.

"Didn't you say you were married and even had children?" he asked curiously.

"We got divorced three years ago," I replied.

"What about your children?"

"Living with my mother."

"Ah well, then it should bother you even less!" He said, smiling cheerfully.

By then, we had already stepped back on the pier. Since the ticket had already been paid for, I obviously could no longer change it. We parted ways at the tram stop.

Two days before my departure, Sherkels called me again, but I was not at home. I was busy all day with social engagements and only went to see him on the evening before the day of the sailing to say my farewells. I expressed my regrets for having missed his calls. He said he had called me twice on Thursday, but I had not been home. On Friday, he had invited his friend's daughter for dinner and he had wanted me to come as well so that the two of us could get to know each other, but he had not been able to find me. He then asked me if I would be free the next day for lunch. I thanked him, but said that I would not be able to make it, to which he replied that we just would have to acquaint ourselves onboard. "Husband and wife on their honeymoon," he added jokingly.

And that's how I became the "husband" of that young lady yet unknown to me who today was wearing a blue and gray dress. I was still blushing, but all my regrets came too late. I felt uneasy, and I feared I would have to endure this unease for the whole month of the journey.

She was extremely vivacious and within a day had met practically everyone on board. When she encountered people on deck, she would introduce them to me: "This is Mr. So-and-So and Mrs. So-and-So; this is my husband."

As for the names of all these So-and-Sos, I could not remember any of them. I am not someone who is good at socializing, and when she introduced me to all those people, I would only mumble a few perfunctory words and then remain silent. She, on the other hand, enthusiastically engaged in conversation, especially with one young Italian. She talked to him endlessly, all the while looking at me, as if she wanted me to be a little jealous or arouse a competitive spirit in me. Her behavior, however, did not have much of an effect on a middle-aged man like me. I had known too many girls like that, and besides, I had too many other things on my mind. What's more, in my mind, I could have been her father's friend, and seeing the photos of her as a child at Sherkels's apartment made me think of her as even younger than she was. For all those reasons, my emotions remained as calm as the sea at the time of our crossing. And, just to make sure I would not even be tempted by her little games, I struck up a conversation with an older gentleman close by.

This in turn made her unhappy. She came over to me and said she needed to go to the cabin to get her binoculars and she wanted me to go with her. I could not refuse her request and so started to walk toward the cabin. She quickly followed me, and once she had caught up linked arms with me and glanced at that young Italian who was just then looking over at us.

When we got to the cabin, she said, "You are my husband now, and you should treat me like your wife."

"But I am only your nominal husband," I replied.

"So what if it's in name only. On the surface, you can still act like a proper husband, don't you think?"

"Even if I were to act like a proper husband, I would still act like a Chinese husband, would I not?" I asked.

"On the surface a Chinese husband might appear less caring of his wife than his Western counterpart, but deep in his heart, a Chinese husband cares a lot more," she replied. "But you …"

"I am not a teenager, you know," I said. "And besides, I have a lot of things on my mind."

"So you think I am still a child?" She asked.

"Of course!" I exclaimed. "I have seen all of those photographs from your childhood at Sherkels's place." This, of course, was only an expression of what I had been thinking, and no evidence of her acting like a child. But she did not refute me. She just smiled and said, "But now I am your wife."

And so, the days passed by. I spent my time just as I would have spent it traveling alone. I read, chatted a little with other people, and played chess. When she wanted to talk with me, I talked to her. When she wanted to be with me, I spent time with her. Otherwise, I left her to her own devices. And even though I would miss her a little after not seeing her for several hours, on the whole I acted with extreme reserve toward her. Waking up early every morning, I would invariably feel that I was ill suited for the role of a nominal husband, which would make me even more frustrated about getting caught up in this whole business. Yet on those evenings when I withdrew to our cabin first, she always followed me down. And on those occasions when she wanted to go down first, she came to get me. Sometimes, when I was sitting in the salon and she wanted to go on deck with some other people to amuse herself—usually that young Italian would be one of them—she asked me to get her when I went down to the cabin. But this always made me uneasy. What if I went to get her and she was in the middle of some amorous adventures? I, her "husband" who never seemed jealous, but who at times could not avoid feeling a little sad, would be embarrassed. That was why I would prefer to wait for her in the salon. Sometimes I would read, at other times I would write a letter, or, if there were other passengers around, I might play chess with one of them.

When we returned to our cabin, she usually wanted to talk to me before going to sleep. She told me stories about the other passengers. She said that the young Italian was a Fascist, but that he was nevertheless courting her in a most romantic way. I said that falling in love is what young people do and that it had nothing to do with Fascism or Communism or the like.

I can't remember when it started, but some time into the journey, she asked me to sit by her side and talk to her after she had lain down for the night on her lower bunk. This soon became a habit. At night, I usually woke up several times, and when I noticed that her blanket had slipped off I put it back over her. I got used to all this as the days went by.

One night, she once more started to talk about that Italian. I said, "He might be genuinely in love with you, and I think you might be in love with him, too."

"I am certainly not in love with him, but I might have fallen in love with you a little."

"Fallen in love with me?" I laughed, attempting to hide my true emotions which, if I were to be frank, amounted to two-thirds being flattered and one third feeling that this was just the typical sweet talk of a young woman.

"I think that you might also love me a little." She was looking away as she said it.

I did not know how to reply. I laughed and said, "You reckon that when a person falls in love with another person, that person can at that very moment understand with clarity his or her own sentiments for what they really are?"

"Maybe you are only secretly in love with me, which is why you don't dare to say it clearly," she said.

"What do you mean by secretly? If I loved you, what would there be to be afraid of?" I asked.

"You can be afraid of things without knowing it. A lot of university professors are secretly in love with their female students, many wealthy men are secretly in love with their maids, many older men are secretly in love with younger women. Only great poets and great artists dare to express this kind of love openly. When Goethe was eighty years old, he fell in love with a young girl. Who doesn't have such feelings? It's just that people don't dare to talk about them," she said.

"You think that in the short span of time that we have spent together, we could have already fallen in love?" I asked.

"Love is the thing of an instant. Sometimes, a friendship lasts for ten years and there is no love, but then suddenly, in the spark of a moment, love is born. And it is the same kind of love as when you fall in love at first sight. You see, there is no correlation between love and time."

At a loss for words, I got up from her bed and went to wash my hands. I took a knife to cut an orange in two, and gave her one half. Seemingly in jest, she suddenly said, "Do you think we would be happy if the two of us were to get married for real?"

"I haven't thought about it," I replied. "Do you think being married to a Chinese man would make you happy?"

"You are not saying that interracial marriages are no good, are you?" She asked.

"That's a Fascist theory. I am not at all of that opinion," I said, and changed the topic.

When I went to bed, I could not fall asleep. I realized that she did in fact love me, but how could she have known that I too loved her? Even I would not have realized it had she not alerted me to it.

And then, over the next two days, the following happened. The wind had grown strong and there was a heavy swell. She got seasick and did not leave her bunk. Usually, I did not impose on her. I would remain aloof and let her socialize with the other passengers. But once she had come down with seasickness, I could not help but sit by her side in our cabin. She was under my watch for two full days, and I could not conceal the happiness that began to show on my face. I dropped my restraint. I had felt compelled to keep my distance when she was with others, but now that it was just the two of us, I no longer felt the need for it. And this was precisely the heart of the matter; for, as long you are in love with another person without yet having realized it, you can still pretend not to be in love. But once you've realized it, pretending is no longer possible. If you have become aware that you are in love, but the other person who in the meantime has also fallen in love does not speak out, it is still possible to show restraint. But once the other person acknowledges that there is mutual love, it all becomes so much harder.

What was there to be done now? Should I admit that I had fallen in love with her? Should I court her or not? And if I decided to court her, how should I go about it? Should I go to Europe with her and then take her back to China? The problem was that my family was all country folk and my father and mother were simple farmers. On the day of my departure, my mother had said to me that under no circumstances should I take a foreign wife. This was a real dilemma: My feet had not even touched foreign soil, and yet I was already married to a foreign woman. What was I to do about it?

I kept turning this question over in my mind. I finally told myself that since we soon would reach Europe anyway, we should quickly take care of her business first. If by then our emotions for each other had cooled, then maybe that was for the better. But if not, then everything should be left to fate. Down in her lower bunk, she was not sleeping either. Again and again I heard her toss and turn, but I had no idea what she was thinking.

Her destination was Naples, and we finally arrived. She spoke Italian and thus everything went smoothly. We first went to look for a hotel. Since we had to keep up the appearance of being a married couple, we naturally stayed in one room. She then said she would go and look for the attorney. Once everything was in place, she would bring me along. But when she came back, she said that the attorney had gone to Rome and would not be back for five days.

"Five days?" I was reluctant to delay my own departure for so long.

"There is nothing to be done about it," she said apologetically. "Would you mind doing this for me? Why don't you use this as an opportunity to enjoy yourself a little?"

On the second day, she did not accompany me but instead told me about some places of interest and how to get there. She then left on her own. I spent the day sightseeing. When I got back to the hotel, she had not yet returned. By the time I took dinner on my own, she still had not returned. Long after dinner, there still was no sign of her. It turned midnight, one o'clock, two o'clock. She finally came back at three o'clock. I was still wide awake when she walked in. She was laughing loudly and I knew she must have been drinking. She sat down on the sofa and began to smoke. She no longer seemed to resemble the person she had been on the ship. She had suddenly changed, but why?

"Catherine," I said sternly.

"How was your day?" she asked me.

"I was just about to ask you the same."

"I was taken out by some friends," she said. "We danced all night. Let's go to sleep, I have to get up early tomorrow to take care of some business."

On the third day, she again told me about some places I could visit and how to get there, but then left again on her own. I spent another day sightseeing. When I got back to the hotel, she had not yet returned. I ate dinner alone at the hotel again, and long after dinner there was still no sign of her. I assumed it would be just like the previous night and went to bed first. But I was unable to fall asleep. I heard a church bell ring at midnight, and again at one, at two.... I must have fallen asleep shortly after two and I did not immediately wake up when she returned. It was only after she had washed herself and changed into her nightgown that she called out my name. To my utter surprise, she suddenly slipped under my blanket. I was wide awake now. I was at a loss and can hardly express what I felt in that moment. I might have felt a little flattered, but for the most part I felt uncomfortable.

Her kiss tasted of alcohol. I did not know what to say and finally asked her, "What is this supposed to mean? Why are you doing this?"

She did not reply, but let out a soft sigh, not of sorrow, it seemed, but rather from fatigue. Her hands and feet were ice cold. I grasped her hands.

"Catherine …" I said.

"If we both believe that we love each other," she replied, "then let us prove our love to each other tonight."

"Haven't we already done that when we both admitted that we are in love with each other?" I asked.

"But …" She embraced me, pressing her body tightly against mine.

"Catherine, I think this is where Chinese and Westerners differ," I said.

"What is that supposed to mean?" she asked.

"What I mean is that the Chinese see physical love as the starting point of love while Westerners see it as the finish line."

"I still don't understand," she said.

"You see, if you and I make love to each other now, I will love you even more; and when we part from each other, I will miss you even more. But you, you are a Westerner, and if you make love to me once, love for you will have borne fruit, and you can forget me. There is a saying in China: for only one night husband and wife, and affection will linger all their life. This really sums up how the Chinese feel about love. The two of us will soon part. You will be able to forget me after this one night we had together, but I will miss you more and more until my last day."

"But …"

"We shouldn't do this. If the two of us are meant to stay together, we can get married for real in the future. What I want to know now is what has been going on for the past two days?"

"You will soon know. Tonight, I want to … but we don't have to. But please tell me, you love me, don't you?"

"If I didn't love you, I would have made love to you just now and tomorrow would have gone my way. It's because I love you, because I value our love, that I don't."

She did not reply, but kissed me violently. The bell in the

nearby clock tower tolled, but her heart beat even louder. In the end, she fell asleep in my arms. As I listened to her soft breathing, questions and worries filled my heart. An unspeakable weight bore down on me. As a matter of fact, with things having come this far, our love needed to be sealed by way of a genuine marriage. Why was I still hesitating? But as far as she was concerned, I felt I understood her less these past two days than I had on the ship. What had she really been up to these past two days? Why did she have to lead a life like this all of a sudden? Of course she probably had friends here, but did she really have to get drunk and come back this late? I simply could not make heads or tails of it. I tried to analyze her behavior from every imaginable angle, but there did not seem to be any satisfactory explanation. I began to slide into darkness. The only way to find out what was really going on, I thought, was to question her again.

But when I woke up the next morning, she was already washing herself and getting ready.

"What's your plan today?" I asked her straight out.

"There still is something that I need to take care of today. Why don't you take a car to Pompeii," she said, as if she had not been sleeping in my embrace last night.

"What's actually been happening to you these past two days? I would like to know!" I demanded.

"Tonight you will know," she said while looking at herself in the mirror.

As I was getting up, she calmly walked over to me, kissed me, and left. That moment, she made me feel like a little child.

I did not follow her recommendation to visit Pompeii. I felt gloomy all morning. I tried to write letters and to read but could not concentrate on either. I did not know how to cheer myself up. After lunch, I went for a walk. My mind was in chaos. I thought of how she had behaved, thought of what had happened last night, and tried to imagine what might be. There weren't many people in the streets at that time. A few trams passed by.

Suddenly, behind the rear window of a black sedan, I saw the shadow of a man and woman. I was stunned. Because the car was stuck behind a slow-moving tram, I could see them clearly. There was no doubt about it: The woman was Catherine, and the man was that Italian from the ship. They were talking and laughing intimately. I wanted to call out to her, but soon the car sped past the tram and disappeared. For an instant, I felt a jealousy I had never experienced in my life before. I could not suppress my anguish. I wanted to call a cab and catch up with them, but what good would that have done? I even thought of killing myself, but that too would have been pointless. There was nothing for me to do but to return to the hotel. I wanted to leave immediately, leave Italy for France, but ultimately gave up on the idea.

I really loved her. I also kept telling myself that I had yet to fulfill my bargain as her nominal husband. Moreover, I simply had to see her one more time. Regardless of what happened afterward, I had to see her one more time. I wistfully returned to my hotel room. Lying on my bed smoking, I waited for the time to pass. After dinner, I no longer could contain my anguish. I inquired about a dance hall, changed, and went out. I forgot myself, got drunk, and amused myself with some French-speaking prostitutes until two in the morning. I returned to the hotel in the same dejected state. When I entered the room, Catherine was sitting on the sofa. Seeing me walk in half-drunk without a word, she got up in surprise and led me to the sofa.

"Xu, what's going on?" she asked.

"What's going on with you?" I replied in anger.

"I can tell you everything now." She took out two cigarettes, one for herself and one for me. She sat on the sofa next to me and appeared extremely calm and composed.

"To tell you the truth, I haven't come here because of an inheritance." She paused for a moment, and then continued: "My father was Jewish and he died during the Great War. My mother is Spanish. She was a famous spy during the war. She disguised herself as a laundry woman working for the army. At the time, I was only six years old and helped her deliver the laundry. Of course my mother did not let me know that she was a spy. She is still alive now and fights in the Spanish Civil War. I don't want to deceive you any longer. I am here to continue her life work. Shipments with ammunition are frequently sent from here to Franco, and I am here to conduct sabotage operations."

I was stunned. At the same time, I was not yet entirely convinced. Did this not sound too much like a story from a spy novel? I therefore asked her, "So why did you need me to come along?"

"Without you, I wouldn't have been able to enter the country. That's why I needed you to become my husband, why we had to sail on the same ship, why we had to withdraw to our cabin together at night, why you had to treat me just like you would treat your real wife. All this was meant as camouflage." She suddenly sounded exhausted and she continued with a tired voice. "I have come here three times already to do this kind of job. This time, it was a deadly mission. I made it through alive, but only because someone who loves me gave his life instead."

"Someone who loves you?" I asked, a little frightened now.

"That's right, but it's not you. It's that young Italian from the ship."

When she had finished, she threw herself in my arms, and exclaimed, now suddenly agitated, "Let's quickly pack. There is a train for France that leaves at five. We have to leave or else terrible things might happen."

In that moment, it felt as if I had turned into the six-year-old her, and she had assumed the role of her mother. I did everything as she said. I had complete faith in her. Two hours later, we found ourselves aboard a train. Approaching France at sixty miles an hour, she finally seemed cheerful again and lightheartedly gazed out of the window. Then she looked at me and smiled, and we chatted a little. A lot of thoughts were running through my mind. I felt like in a dream. The whole world around me, it seemed, had changed colors. There were still many things about her and about her mission that I did not understand. I wanted to ask a lot of questions but sensed that she probably did not want to talk about these things now. But when the train had finally crossed into France, I could no longer hold back.

"If you only needed me to bring you into the country, then why did you want me stay behind with you?" I asked.

"Didn't I also need you to get me out of the country? Look, I don't want to lie to you anymore. According to my original plan, if at some point someone would have had to die, I probably would have sacrificed you. But then I fell in love with you and, because of the sincerity of your feelings during our voyage, I could never have brought myself to do it. On that evening, when it became clear that someone would have to die, the evening I slept in your embrace, I could not decide whether you would die for me or I would die for you. I could no longer bear to think about it, but no matter what, I wanted us to consummate our marriage. But then, I suddenly thought of him...."

"So you and Sherkels had actually planned on sacrificing me...."

"Yes, but don't blame him. You yourself probably would have thought of sacrificing yourself, just as I would have done the same. What's the weight of one of us compared to the weight of the suffering of the Spanish people?"

I did not say anything, but silently adored her.

All the papers in Paris already carried the news about her big coup. They also mentioned the young Italian who had died in her place and who was turned into a hero. I sent news of our real marriage to Sherkels, and for a week, the two of us experienced heaven on earth. In my current state of mind, I do not have the strength to talk about just how happy we were. It simply would cause me too much grief. One week later, she left for Germany. I obviously had no right to stand in the way of that great cause of hers. After I saw her off at the station, all that remained was the image of her waving at me from the train. In that image, she appeared strong and vigorous, lively, happy, courageous, and nimble. I soon succumbed to a numb yearning for her that left me depressed and fearful. My fear and my longing for her grew stronger each day until it completely overwhelmed me. But there was no word from her.

Not long after, there was some frightening news in the papers. I knew in my heart that it must have been about her, but still I kept waiting for word from her.

Finally, word came in the form of a letter from Sherkels. It was simple, yet stirring:

Her love and beauty, her spirit and flesh were a bright torch that burned for this world!

Yes, she was light, she was fire; she was a star that gave its luster and warmth for mankind, a comet that perished in a sea of clouds.

May 15, 1937. Paris, deep in the night.

鳥語
Bird Talk

"Bird Talk" was among the first new works of fiction that Xu Xu published after arriving in Hong Kong. When it became apparent that his legacy as a writer of exotic romances would sooner or later become a political liability in the newly founded People's Republic, Xu Xu decided to leave mainland China for what he thought would only be a temporary exile.

While the foreign concessions of Shanghai had been returned to Chinese jurisdiction at the end of World War II, Hong Kong, which had been occupied by the Japanese in the wake of Pearl Harbor, was not returned to China but to its former colonial power, Great Britain. It soon became the destination for millions of Chinese who were displaced by the civil war between the Communists and the Nationalists that had flared up again after Japan's surrender. For some, Hong Kong was just a stepping stone on their journey to either Taiwan, other parts of Asia, or the United States. Others, and Xu Xu would ultimately be one of them, reluctantly made Hong Kong their new home. By the end of 1950, almost two million refugees had arrived in Hong Kong, and, over the next two decades, several hundred thousand more would follow.

The founding of a new China by Mao Zedong in 1949 had signaled the end of the Republican period (1912–49), and 1950 marked a watershed in Xu Xu's life and in the lives of those Chinese who had left their homes and families in the mainland—Xu Xu himself became separated from his second wife and daughter after settling in Hong Kong. Something irretrievable was lost, it seemed, and, unsurprisingly, nostalgia became a common theme in the literature and film of the period. The narrator in "Bird Talk," however, also seems to be in search of something more elusive than a lost home and appears to have gotten a glimpse of it through the story's protagonist.

The story opens in postwar Hong Kong, where the narrator receives news concerning a certain *Juening 覺寧. From the Chinese characters, it is clear that Juening is a dharma name or Buddhist name of religion that literally translates as Peaceful Awareness. Much of the narrative that follows is a flashback that takes the reader first to the idyllic beauty of the prewar Chinese countryside, somewhere in the lush rice-growing expanses south of the Yangtze River, and later to the bustling city of Shanghai.

The *Three Hundred Tang Poems 唐詩三百首 that the narrator uses to teach the protagonist is a popular anthology of some of the best-loved poems from the Tang dynasty (618–907). Compiled during the Qing dynasty (1644–1912), it includes works by poets such as Du Fu 杜甫, Li Bai 李白, Wang Wei 王維, Bai Juyi 白居易 and many more. *Jessfield Park was a public garden near Shanghai's International Settlement that had been established in 1914. Its Chinese name was Zhaofeng Park 兆豐公園. In 1944, it was renamed Zhongshan Park 中山公園, in honor of the founder of the Republic of China, Dr. Sun Yatsen (1866–1925), who is also known as Sun Zhongshan. The park is still called Zhongshan Park today.

When I opened the parcel that had just arrived in the mail I found that it contained a copy of the Diamond Sutra. It was a large and very elaborate woodblock edition printed on exquisite paper. The handwriting on the parcel was unfamiliar, but from the postmark I could see that it had been sent from my maternal grandmother's village. I was dumbstruck. In my bewilderment, I began to flip through the pages, gazing at the red punctuation marks. As I impatiently awaited the arrival of more news, I was overcome by a troubling feeling of anxiety and fear that began to unsettle my normal life.

After six days, I received a simple letter that bore the same postmark. The handwriting again was unfamiliar and the letter itself was brief. "On the fifth day of the eight month of the lunar calendar," it read, "Sister *Juening departed to wander among the immortals. Just before she passed away, she asked us to send you a copy of the Diamond Sutra."

So she had died! It was a dreary autumn night. I was sitting at my desk under the glare of an electric light and stared at the coarse paper with its childish, hastily scribbled handwriting until my eyes began to blur. There was a mirror on my desk, and when I saw myself in its reflection, it seemed as if my life of the past many years unfolded in front of me. It was a round mirror and, through my tear-stained eyes, its surface rippled, momentarily turning into a small pond. I was sitting on a white rock next to the pond. Staring at my tired face in the water's reflection, I said to myself:

"What is gone is gone, errors cannot be undone, what is lost is lost, what has vanished cannot be brought back."

* * *

"Breakfast is ready! Your grandma asked me to call you."

The silhouette of a girl appeared by the side of the pond. Her face was round and thin, and she had braids falling on each shoulder. She wore a patterned cotton shirt with rolled-up sleeves, gray trousers, and no socks. Her naked white shins were stuck in a pair of black cotton shoes that were damp from the dew on the grass. I don't know why, but I touched her shoes with my hand and said, "Your shoes are all wet!"

She was taken aback, turned around, and ran away. I got up. Gazing at her vanishing figure, I wondered who she was. It had been a week since my arrival at Huilan Village. How come I had never run into her before? Who was this beautiful girl? At the breakfast table, I asked grandma.

"A dimwit," she said.

"A dimwit?" I was stunned. "Such a pretty girl?"

"An embroidered pillow," grandma said. "Pretty only on the outside."

"How come I haven't run into her before?"

"She doesn't like to interact with people, and usually hides herself away."

I wanted to ask more, but just then someone came in and asked to borrow something from grandma, and so our conversation was cut short. I did not see the girl after that and forgot all about her.

II

Many years ago, in 19xx, I was suffering from a serious case of mental exhaustion. My heart was racing and I had insomnia. Moreover, I felt depressed and often found myself talking to myself. My doctor told me that I should find a quiet place in the countryside, and my mother suggested that I go to Huilan Village, where my maternal grandmother lived, and stay there for a few months. It was a small village south of the Yangtze River, consisting of no more than a dozen households. In front of the village there was a threshing ground covered with grass and surrounded by trees. The hills that rose behind seemed close on clear days and distant when it was cloudy. A small river flowed a few hundred steps from the village, and if you traveled it by boat or walked along its banks for about two to three miles, you reached a market town. Most of the villagers were farmers, and they all lived quiet and simple lives.

In the back of my grandma's house was a large garden with a bamboo thicket. There were also some fruit trees, and shrubs of wild flowers. It was surrounded by a rickety bamboo fence. In the middle stood an elegant old-style pavilion. In bygone days, this garden would probably have been a flower garden, and the pavilion a place to drink wine, admire flowers, and compose poetry. But no one engages in such refined activities anymore, so grandma used it as storage for farming tools and other objects.

When grandma heard that I was going to stay with her, she prepared a room for me in a wing of the house that faced the front courtyard. The courtyard was bordered by the neighboring households. All day, people walked in and out and children were playing inside the yard. Bothered by the hustle and bustle, I asked grandma if I could move into the pavilion in the garden. She asked if I would not be scared at night all alone in the pavilion, but I told her that I was not afraid of ghosts. And so, after she had the room swept for me, the walls whitewashed, and things put in order, I moved into the pavilion in the garden. My move caused no small amount of amazement among the neighbors. They all thought it rather odd that I did not want to be together with everyone else and instead preferred to live on my own in a secluded corner.

When I arrived at my grandma's I was determined to follow my doctor's orders. I went to bed early and even when I could not fall asleep would lie in bed and read. When I still was unable to fall asleep, I would take a sleeping pill. In the morning, I went out for walks and then had breakfast upon my return. I would take a nap after lunch and in the afternoon a hot bath. After that, I went out again and walked for a quarter of a mile or so before dinner. After dinner, older women from the neighboring villages stopped by my grandma's place. I would listen to their chattering for a while and then retire to bed. In that way, my days passed quite agreeably. I gradually got to know the people in the village, all of whom were decent country folk. Among them was a certain Li Bingyang. He was a little over thirty and had a calm and composed nature. He enjoyed playing chess, and it turned out that he and I were a good match. He liked to come over for a game and soon we got to know each other quite well.

III

It felt rather peculiar on the first morning after I moved into the pavilion. While staying in the front room facing the yard, all I had heard in the morning was people's voices. In the back, however, all I heard was the singing of countless birds that were flying in and out of the bamboo thicket. As the first rays of the sun shone into the garden, a gentle breeze stroked the leaves of the bamboo. It was spring, and the air was crisp and clean. I got up and went into the garden. I took a deep breath and looked at the world that surrounded me. Suddenly, I saw the shadow of a person next to the rickety bamboo fence. It was a girl, and she was squatting on the other side, facing the bamboo thicket inside the garden. Just when I wanted to take a closer look, she noticed me, got up, and ran away. I did not give this encounter another thought, but the next day, after I had gotten up and opened the window to gaze outside, I noticed her again. It seemed as if from amidst the chirping and trilling, she herself was making crooning sounds. I kept looking at her, and even though I was curious, I did not go outside for fear of startling her. From then on, I saw her practically every morning. I became determined to find out what she was actually up to, and after eight or nine days of observing her I rose early one morning, even before the birds had begun to sing. The sky was not yet completely light, and I went into the garden to find a place that was close enough to the fence where she usually stood, yet also hidden by the bamboo thicket. Then I waited for her.

It was a hazy morning. The sky was colorless except for a faint red glow in the east. Soon, the birds in the bamboo thicket started to sing. At first, there was only one, chirping away in a clear and captivating way and flying from branch to branch. Another one began to sing, as if answering the other. Just then, I heard a response from beyond the fence and I caught sight of the girl, wearing a gray dress, her hair done up in two braids. A chorus of birds began chirping away from inside the bamboo thicket. The two birds that had sung to each other flew to the fence and began trilling at the girl on the other side. The girl raised her head. Her face was round, and her eyes shone brightly. She bore a happy smile. The sounds she was making were beautiful. They neither sounded like the trilling of birds, nor did they sound like singing. The girl and the two birds seemed like old acquaintances. The birds flew back and forth between the fence and her shoulder and then landed on the fence and chirped affectionately. By then, the morning haze had already disappeared, and the sun shone onto the dewy grass. I was able to see the girl's face clearer now. Her chin was pointed, and she had thin lips, a delicate nose, and a broad forehead. Her eyes were radiant. What was most astonishing was her skin. It seemed as if it had rarely been exposed to the sun. It was of a very light complexion, like porcelain, not at all like that of other country folk. Suddenly a bird flew into the bamboo thicket. Had it noticed me? It called out from the inside and then came flying out again. I could see that the girl was looking straight at me now, and I thought it best to come forward and greet her.

I took a few quick steps toward the fence and, slightly bowing toward her, said, "Good morning."

She abruptly turned around to run away, but then, as if she wanted to look me over, halted for a moment. And so I said, "You don't need to be afraid, I live here. You know me, don't you?"

She was relatively composed now, and looked at me again.

All of a sudden she giggled, turned around, and ran away. "I'll wait for you tomorrow morning," I shouted. "We'll listen to the birds together."

IV

Who was she? In the afternoon, while grandma was shelling dried beans, I sat down beside her and began to ask about the girl.

"She's that dimwit," grandma said. "Poor soul."

"You mean she's the one who called me for breakfast the other day?" I asked. "How come I never saw her afterward?"

"She doesn't like to mix with people, and doesn't really have anyone looking after her. There isn't much her elder brother can do, either."

"Who is her brother?"

"It's Bingyang, the fellow who often plays chess with you."

"What about their parents?"

"They are both dead," grandma said.

"So there is only the two of them?"

"Bingyang got married two years ago," grandma said. "You have seen his wife, haven't you? She's pretty and quite capable. They also have a child."

"What's the girl's name? And does she live with her brother and his wife?"

Living under one roof with a pretty and astute sister-in-law surely cannot be easy, I immediately thought.

"She is named Yunqian."

My grandma was an extremely perceptive and wise old lady, and she right away could sense that I had taken pity on Yunqian. She smiled at me kindly and said, "Her sister-in-law treats her very well."

"How come they don't send her to school? What's their financial situation?"

"Bingyang has two shops in town," grandma said. "But Yunqian is just too dumb. She struggled all throughout primary school and only graduated last year. That's why Bingyang no longer sends her to school."

"Dumb?" I said incredulously. "You wouldn't guess that from her face."

"She is an embroidered pillow!" grandma said. "Look, she is seventeen this year and can barely read. She is incapable of doing needlework and doesn't understand a thing. You have to poke her if you want her to do anything, just like a child of six or seven. What's more, she doesn't like to talk and cannot express herself clearly. When her mother was still alive, she didn't know what to do with her."

"She seems to like birds," I said.

"That's true. She has liked birds since she was a child. The moment she'd see a sparrow or a magpie or a swallow, she'd make some foolish chirping sounds at them. Now she is seventeen and she is still like that. She is acting a little more normal now, but only because everyone laughs at her. In secret she still sneaks out to look at birds."

Auntie Wang who lived next door and who had seen that grandma was shelling beans came over to give us a hand. She sat down and said, "You're talking about the dimwit, aren't you?"

"Why do you call her that?" I felt rather uneasy.

"Everyone here calls her that," grandma said.

"A couple of days ago," auntie Wang continued, "they asked someone to act as a go-between. I hear the boy was from a good family, but once they realized she was a dimwit that was the end of it."

"She herself probably doesn't want to get married," grandma said. "I mean, a seventeen year old who acts as if she is thirteen or fourteen ..."

"She'll still be this way when she's sixty. A dimwit like her simply won't grow up," auntie Wang said.

"And even if she got married, it wouldn't be easy for her either," grandma said. "Poor soul!"

"But what will she do if she doesn't get married? Surely she can't rely on her brother all her life," auntie Wang exclaimed.

Hearing them talk like this made me extremely uncomfortable, and so I quietly left.

V

The fence around the garden was dilapidated, but it was still standing. There was a single-leaf gate at the southern corner of the fence with a coarse iron lock, the kind they use in the countryside. The key hung on the back wall of my pavilion. The next day, I rose early again and went to unlock the gate. Then I waited next to the gate for Yunqian. The place was quite a distance from where I had waited for her the previous day. The weather that day was marvelous. There was no morning haze, and white clouds drifted in the dark-blue sky. The faint contours of the moon were still visible and, in the east, the sun began to rise, slowly jolting upward like a big red ball. Before long, Yunqian arrived. Like the previous day, she stood on the other side of the fence, gazing at the birds inside the garden. She neither seemed aware of my presence nor did she seem to remember that I was awaiting her, and I did not step forward to greet her. The birds were already singing, but Yunqian did not make a sound; she just stood there. Her face was radiating happiness. After a while, she started to trill in a low voice and two birds flew over to her. She squatted down and chirped away with them for a while. Then those two birds flew away and two more flew over. More and more birds began to chirp until eventually flock after flock took off and flew away. I tiptoed toward the fence and saw her waving at the parting birds. From across the fence, I softly called out to her:

"Yunqian."

She turned around. It seemed as if she suddenly remembered

what I had said the previous day and a shy, intelligent smile appeared on her face.

"Yunqian," I said, "I think I understand you, just like you understand those birds."

She did not pay any attention to me. I thought she was going to run away again, but somehow her curiosity seemed to pull her back. "Don't run," I said. "I wish you'd think of me as just another bird and talk to me just like you do to them. You know that I am staying with my grandmother to get over an illness, don't you?"

She did not run away, but she did not say anything either. The smile on her face was no longer shy, but now showed astonishment. She knit her brows, and I saw an unusual beauty and nobility in her face.

"Why don't you come into the garden? There are a lot of things I want to tell you."

She did not move, and I said, "Well, then I'll come out."

She suddenly smiled, and, with the same artlessness with which she had been conversing with the birds, said, "Why don't we just talk like this?"

"I just want you to think of me as a bird, not a human," I said. "My heart is that of a bird." She nodded her head and smiled cheerfully.

"You can understand bird talk," I said. "I hope you can teach me."

"How do you know?" she asked. "No one here believes me."

"I know they don't, but I do," I said, "because my heart is that of a bird."

"But you don't understand them."

"No, I don't understand them, but that's because I am too stupid."

"No," she suddenly said, as if pitying me. "You are definitely not stupid. You know that I am a dimwit, don't you?"

"You shouldn't listen to what people say," I said to her.

"Everything other people can do you can easily learn, but what you know, no one else can learn."

"But I can't read, I can't get things done, and they say I can't express myself clearly."

"That's not true," I said. "If you want to read, I can teach you. You'll see that it's not hard at all. All it takes is following some rules and being diligent."

"You will teach me?" she asked excitedly.

"Of course," I said. "I don't have anything to do. Look, if you like, I can talk to your brother tomorrow. I'll teach you how to read, and you teach me bird talk."

But then she suddenly said with a nervous tone, "I honestly don't know how to teach you bird talk."

"No need to worry," I said. "I am not saying you have to teach me. Even if you can't teach me, I can still teach you how to read, right? I don't have anything else to do."

"Really? Then I will ask my brother later." But then she looked dejected again and said, "I am sure you'll think I am too stupid."

"Nonsense!" I said. "And even if you are stupid, what of it? Don't you know that I am all the more stupid?"

"Do you know that all my primary school teachers hated me?"

"But those birds that just left, do they hate you?" I asked her.

"No."

"And you still don't believe that my heart is that of a bird?"

Her smile returned, and she softly said, "I will talk to my brother later. I am leaving now."

I gazed at her beautiful silhouette disappearing in the distance. Once or twice, she turned around to look at me. I waved at her, just as she had waved at those departing birds before.

VI

I thought that Bingyang would come and see me, but when the sun descended in the west and dusk began to fall, he still had not shown up.

Over dinner, my grandma suddenly said, "That Bingyang is an odd fellow. What made him think you'd want to teach his sister how to read?"

"What? He talked to you?" I asked.

"Yes, he specially came over to talk to me. I said you have come here to convalesce and that you wouldn't be interested. That dimwit, there is no use in teaching her anyway," grandma said flatly.

"But I'd be more than happy to teach her." I said.

"Your mother told you to come here to recuperate. You should relax, get plenty of sleep, and eat well. Isn't that also what the doctor told you to do?"

"But teaching her how to read won't be much of an effort. Those couple of hours each day will distract me a little. I don't have anything else to do and I am getting a little bored."

"Well, if it makes you happy, I will tell them tomorrow."

"How about you go tonight," I said, "I can start teaching her tomorrow morning at ten. Every day from ten till noon, what do you think?"

"You might as well, I guess," grandma replied. "And you can of course stop anytime if you no longer feel like teaching her."

After dinner, grandma sent someone over to inform Bingyang that she had discussed everything with me and that it was decided that we would start tomorrow morning. I would teach Yunqian every day from ten till noon.

Early the next morning, I again went to meet Yunqian in the back of the garden. Just like the day before, I waited until the birds had left the bamboo thicket before I spoke to her. I asked her to come inside the garden, but she didn't want to. I then asked whether she was coming back at ten to study with me, but she abruptly said, "My brother said that your grandma told him that you are here to convalesce. He feels bad about disturbing you."

"Nonsense," I said. "Teaching you for a couple of hours a day would be a welcome distraction for me. Promise me that you will talk to your brother. I am really happy to teach you."

"But I haven't told him that we have been meeting here in the mornings," she said.

I thought about it for a moment, then replied, "That's all right. How about you tell your brother that I want to play a game of chess with him? Tell him I am waiting for him in the afternoon."

She nodded.

"When he comes, I will talk to him myself."

"But please don't tell him anything about what we discussed here."

"Don't worry," I said.

She fell silent and faintly smiled at me. Her face shone with the same happy expression as before, when she had been with the birds. Her eyes avoided my gaze, but their radiance possessed an unfathomable mystery that penetrated my heart and soul. Her lips trembled a little and she bit them with her white, pearl-like teeth, as if there were things she wanted to tell me but could not find the right words. I felt a strange urge to learn more about her. I wanted to ask her about her brother and whether she got along with her sister-in-law, but I did not know how to start. After a while I said, "Why don't we sit in the garden for a while?"

"No," she said. "I have to go back. They'll be looking for me soon." And so she hurried away.

VII

Over our many games of chess, I had learned from Bingyang

that he had attended college for a year, but when his father died he had returned to his village to take care of the shops that his father had left him. He also kept bees and grew fruit. He seemed content with his situation and no longer held lofty ambitions. He was intelligent, levelheaded, and people trusted him with all sorts of matters, but it was also said that he feared his wife. I had seen Bingyang's wife several times. She was a good-looking woman who talked a lot and who acted friendly to everyone, but you could tell right away that it was not sincere. I had never paid much attention to her, but after I had learned that she was Yunqian's sister-in-law, I would exchange a few sentences with her whenever I saw her. She appeared generous on the outside and was certainly very capable, but I felt she was petty, narrow-minded, and a little vulgar. Yunqian could not possibly be happy living under one roof with her, I thought, and Bingyang was probably not very happy, either. Despite our many chats over chess, Bingyang never spoke to me about his wife or his family life. He also never mentioned his younger sister to me. That day, after we had played two games of chess, I casually brought up the topic of teaching Yunqian.

"Didn't you discuss with my grandmother that I was going to tutor your sister a little?"

"I wanted to talk to your grandmother now," he said. "I am afraid it's going to be exhausting for you, why don't we …"

"Come on, what's exhausting about it?" I brushed him off. "My grandmother means well, but I am not that ill, and being on my own all day is actually pretty boring."

"Let me be honest with you," he said. "My sister really is a little dumb."

"I don't believe that the sister of someone like you can possibly be dumb," I said.

"I find it strange myself," he said with a sigh. "There was nothing wrong with my parents. How could she turn out this way? You know, in primary school she was never able to advance to the next grade. Her teachers all said there was nothing anyone could do."

"But she is diligent, is she not?" I asked.

"Extremely diligent! But somehow she …"

"Don't think of her in this way," I said. "Everyone's different. Maybe she just never learned how to stay focused. I think maybe … anyway, let me give it a try. I really would love to find out what is really going on with her. I've seen her a couple of times now, and I am quite sure she isn't the kind of dimwit other people make her to be."

"I sometimes think that, too," Bingyang said. "It's just that she seems incapable of doing anything, even the easiest of household chores."

"I think her present environment might have shattered all her confidence," I said. "Once a person has lost confidence, things go from bad to worse. You know, I myself have had that kind of experience."

"Maybe." His tone suddenly changed. "You know, when my mother was still around she doted on Yunqian. I also wanted to send her to a school in the city, so that she could broaden her horizons, but somehow Yunqian doesn't want to leave here."

"You mean she doesn't want to go the city on her own for school?" I asked.

"Truth is, her experience at primary school terrified her," Bingyang replied. "I simply can't see her studying together with other students anymore."

"That's odd," I said. "How does your wife feel about all this?"

"She feels like any other woman would. Yunqian just hangs around at home and cannot help at all. Now that she is an adult, my wife naturally hopes that she'll get married soon. But I feel uneasy about marrying her off into another family. I know she'd suffer. Even though she looks like a grown woman, her character and temper are those of a child."

"Then let her study with me," I said. "And I can slowly

persuade her to go to the city for more schooling. Here in the countryside, everyone calls her a dimwit, and you and your wife are in no position to help her."

"But it's too much trouble for you," Bingyang insisted.

"Don't worry about that," I said. "I have only seen her a couple of times, but I know that we'll get along."

"Even though she is a little slow, she is really a very fine and honest child," Bingyang suddenly said. "She is eager to help me with anything, but because she is so slow and clumsy, my wife doesn't want her to. When I catch a cold, she'll sit by the side of my bed and won't move an inch, but my wife hates her behaving like this. Says she's putting on a show. Anyway, a lot of women are like that...."

I had thought it somewhat odd that a man of Bingyang's age could at times appear so listless and passive, but now I realized that my initial guess had been right: He certainly wasn't happy, and Yunqian was probably even more troubled. Bingyang loved his younger sister, but he could no longer protect her. Even though he said he wanted Yunqian to go on studying and that it was Yunqian who did not want to leave, who knew whether it wasn't his wife who was making things difficult? His wife naturally wanted Yunqian to marry as soon as possible. Schooling would require tuition and she probably worried about the cost. I left it at that, and we agreed that Yunqian would come over for her first class the next day at ten. Our long conversation had put Bingyang into a gloomy mood, and so we played another round of chess. When he got up to leave, I asked what textbooks Yunqian had used. He said they had some old textbooks at home and that he would ask Yunqian to bring them along tomorrow.

VIII

And that was how I began to teach Yunqian. I had once studied a little pedagogy and child psychology, and I had also taught for several years at a middle school, but Yunqian certainly proved to be a strangely difficult case. I soon was at my wits' end. Whether it was Chinese, arithmetic, natural science, history, or geography, no matter how carefully I explained, she just would not understand any of it. Her expression never assumed that radiance that I had seen when she was listening to birds. She just gazed at me in a stupor. At times I almost thought she was not listening to me. I would ask her to explain to me in her own words what we had studied, one sentence at a time. The parts she was not able to reproduce, I would explain again, but even if she was able to repeat to me what I had explained to her, she still did not understand the meaning of what she said. More than once I almost lost my temper, but I immediately checked myself and did my utmost to encourage her and to keep my own confidence in her. She definitely was not the dimwit everybody made her out to be. There clearly was something special about her; I just had not yet discovered it.

After five days, I added an extra hour of study in the afternoon. Whenever she wasn't able to grasp a new topic, I would try to channel the information to her bit by bit, using all sorts of stories or allegories. In that way, ten days went by. As for the coursework we were trying to tackle, it is fair to say that we did not make much progress, but we managed to get to know each other better and began to interact in a very natural way. In the mornings, she always would come to listen to the birds from the other side of the fence. Only when the birds had flown away would I go out and greet her. Sometimes I would invite her to come into the garden and we would talk about what we had studied the previous day. On other occasions, we would chat about the nearby hills or local stories and legends. She then would return home before showing up promptly at ten, and then again in the afternoon or early evening. She was now much more natural with me than before, but, once we started class, she would be at a loss again. This was a problem I continued to grapple with and I kept wondering how I could possibly get her to view our class as an extension of our everyday conversations, so that she could be as relaxed when studying as she was at other times.

One morning, after we had finished listening to the birds, I met her at the back gate and took her for a walk. It was overcast that day and layer upon layer of gray clouds concealed the sky. The nearby hills appeared distant that day, their contours faint, like in a Chinese landscape painting. The rice paddies had just been planted with new seedlings, and they were rippling like a gentle emerald sea when the wind blew over them, filling the eyes with an expanse of lush green. Dew still covered the path, and our shoes and socks got a little wet. Suddenly, a magpie started to sing from atop of a pine tree. Yunqian stopped to look at it. Her face shone with a radiance that it never showed when we were studying.

I jokingly said, "Yunqian, I have been teaching you for over ten days now and you still haven't taught me any bird talk."

"Bird talk?" She laughed, and then suddenly blurted, "Yes, they seem to be talking, but they are not actually talking."

"They are not talking?" I asked. "But you understand what it is that they are saying?"

"Yes, I understand," she replied, "but I don't quite know how to put it into words."

"Well, what was the meaning of what the magpie just said?" I asked.

"She said … Well, she said …" She began to stutter. "She doesn't mean things the way we do."

"But if there is life, then there is always meaning," I said to her. "The magpie is also a living creature and like other living creatures has to eat and sleep and look for a mate."

"Maybe, maybe …" She knitted her brows and was struggling to find the right words. "But they are different from us, they are not like us.… How can I put this? What I'm trying to say is, their lives are not complicated like ours. They don't need to mean things like we do."

She tried hard to express herself. I could see that she was

very agitated, and I did not dare to ask any further. I was thinking that if bird talk was like a foreign language, then it should be possible to translate it. Could it be that it was not a language but rather a set of symbols in the way an exclamation mark is a symbol? It was of course because Yunqian was unable to translate bird talk that no one in the village believed that she could understand birds. But to me, there was no doubt that Yunqian and the birds were interacting.

I asked her, "How did you learn bird talk?"

"I don't know," she said. "I've just understood it ever since I got to know them."

After a while, I asked, "Do you know if all those birds are happy?"

"Some are, some aren't," she said. "Sometimes they are happy, sometimes they are not."

"The ones who are not, do you comfort them?" I asked.

"Of course I do!"

"So what do you say to them?"

"I can't explain; I just, just …"

There wasn't anything left for me to ask. I realized then that she was bestowed with an unusual gift and that there was no way for me to ever really understand it.

IX

But then one day, something unexpected happened.

That day, my grandma asked me to write a letter for her. When Yunqian came by in the morning, I told her to wait for me in the pavilion and to read for a while. When I returned to my room after ten minutes, she was holding a piece of paper, her face all radiant.

"What's this?" she asked me.

I saw that it was the draft of a poem I had written the previous night:

"Bird Talk"

As the dust rises from the town's street corners
The partridges in the hills
Warbling away in their unperturbed murmurs.

On a tree in the garden under the sun's warm rays,
a senile old woodpecker
talks about nothing but the good old days.

And on top of the willows, from morning 'til sundown
a flock of orioles
singing of spring in the nearby market town.

Nesting under the eaves in many a great number
the little sparrows
chirping about the spring breeze, sunshine, and thunder.

In his cage under a curtain, who is still missing?
The gossipy parrot
complaining about cats and dogs and the tea kettle's
hissing.

Perching on telephone lines that crisscross the land,
Shall we keep listening to man's foolish rant,
Or better just fly away now for they'll never understand?

"It's a poem. I wrote it last night." I said.
"You wrote it?" she asked, her face still radiant. "I like it; can
I make a copy?"
"Of course you can," I said and, suddenly feeling curious, I
asked, "Did you understand what it said?"
"I am not sure," she replied, "but I like it."
"Have you read other poems before?"

"No."

I happened to have a copy of the *Three Hundred Tang Poems* on hand and quickly selected a few poems, which I read out to her. To my utter surprise, she was delighted and that radiance returned to her face. It seemed that she intuitively grasped the poetic beauty of the lines we had just read. Her excitement exhilarated me. I felt I had finally found what spoke to her. That day, all we did was read a few more Tang poems. I asked her which ones she liked and which ones she did not like, and she confidently voiced her clear preferences and dislikes. The whole time, her face bore a happy expression. Her eyes shone brightly with the same radiance that they showed when she was conversing with birds and that was so very different from the dull expression she usually bore during our classes. How I would have loved for that radiance to always shine on her beautiful face!

I did not know what it was that made her grasp the sentiment of each poem. What I read out to her was the literal meaning of the words, but the beauty of a poem often is something that eludes explanation. Her vocabulary naturally was limited, and her compositions frequently lacked cohesion. What's more, her spelling was very poor. Yet with the help of my explanations she effortlessly overcame all the difficulties those poems presented and immediately grasped their poetic qualities. What was most extraordinary, though, was that, while she usually had a hard time remembering our class work, she was able to recite from memory almost all of the lines from the poems, even though we had only read them out loud three or four times. When she went home at noon, I asked her to copy those poems into her notebook. She also borrowed a draft copy of my poem "Bird Talk," and I reminded her to pay attention to the way each word was spelled so that next time she would not misspell them.

The following morning, after we had listened to the birds, we went for a walk. She recited the Tang poems we had read the previous day from memory as well as "Bird Talk." Yet what amazed me most was the indescribable beauty with which she intoned the poems. Especially when reciting "Bird Talk," it felt as if she was endowing the work with new qualities beyond the actual lines I had written.

We happened to be walking toward a white stone tomb of the kind often found south of the Yangtze River, with a sacrificial platform in front of it that was surrounded by a circular stone railing.

When we walked onto the platform, I inadvertently brushed against her porcelain-white hand and, taking hold of it, said to her, "Yunqian." But I no longer knew what I wanted to say.

It was late spring. The sky was blue, the fields were green, and a host of yellow and purple wildflowers surrounded the tomb.

"Do you like spring?" I eventually asked her.

"I do, I like spring a lot, because of the birds and the flowers." As she said so, she briskly shook off my hand and ran off to pick some wildflowers. I did not say anything else. I sat down on the stone railing and thought that she was indeed a mysterious creature, and maybe not of this human world. When she returned, I asked her to sit with me. Beginning with flowers, I told her about botany and about the basic facts surrounding the weather and its connection to plants. Then, looking up at the sky, I told her about the sun and the relationship between the earth and the stars, and about storms and thunder and lightning. Next, I talked about the earth, about geography, and the history of mankind. During this long conversation, I noticed that even though she did not understand everything, she seemed very interested.

The sun was rising toward its zenith. We were bathed in sunlight and I started to feel hot. I realized that we had not had breakfast yet.

"Do you know that we were going over school work just now?" I asked her.

"That was all really interesting."

"Why don't you think about all the things I just told you now. We won't be having another class today," I said, "but you later can show me the poems you copied yesterday."

X

From that day, I no longer clung to a rigid lesson format. Instead, I encouraged her to think for herself, to experiment freely, to try to figure things out by herself. I also shared my poems with her and asked her what she thought of them. Once I was certain that she had understood them, I would ask her whether she liked or disliked them, or whether she agreed or disagreed with me over the meaning of a certain image. Only then would I ask her to try to use her own words to write down her feelings about them. I told her that she did not have to stick to a certain topic or length, and that she should simply write down what she saw and felt. This kind of exercise worked really well for her. She came up with some exceptionally insightful opinions and ideas, and I then helped her with diction and style. In that way, she slowly learned how to express her opinions in writing, even though when stitching together the various pieces into a longer essay, there would invariably be some repetition and inverted logic.

Mathematics was the subject that most puzzled me. She continued to have a hard time with even the simplest of calculations. Regardless of whether she was adding or subtracting, multiplying or dividing, if the numbers were just a little larger, she would not be able to handle them. Very complex mathematical problems, on the other hand, she often was able to think through with relative ease. Hereafter, I no longer insisted that she complete anything that required excessive effort on her part. I wanted her to be confident, to feel unrestrained and natural, not only in our studies, but, I hoped, in her dealings with others. And she certainly showed a lot of improvement. I noticed that even though her cognitive abilities no doubt exceeded those of other people and she had a keen intuition, she was unsystematic and unorganized. She did not have a good memory, yet she possessed an excessive sensibility. She had a dozen souls, but she seemed to lack a brain. Maybe that was precisely why she was of such a sublime and beautiful nature, and why she was so pure and noble.

And so, the days went by. The sea of green rice seedlings had gradually turned into an expanse of golden ears and the weather had started to turn hot. My health had improved greatly. My appetite had increased and I slept better. I experienced an unprecedented peace of mind. My life followed a strict routine, and spending time with Yunqian was not in the least burdensome. I had finally begun to understand her, and she had started to trust me. But then one day in early summer, something strange happened. Usually, Yunqian left just before lunch, but that day, she was still with me when I was getting ready to eat. She walked with me into the house where the table had already been laid, but as I sat down, she ran away without a word. My grandma could not make sense of it, but I immediately sensed that something must have happened. Was it that we had not asked her to stay for lunch? But that was not the custom in the village, and she had never taken lunch with us. I did not say anything, but I began to feel gloomy and uneasy.

The next day, I got up early. I was hoping to ask her about it in the garden, but even though I waited for a long time, there was no trace of her. When she did not show up to class at ten o'clock, I was overcome by a feeling of emptiness and started to worry. Meeting with her all these days, I had not felt anything special, but now that I did not see her for one day I realized how important a part of my life she had become. I could not eat anything for lunch, and was not able to take my afternoon nap. At three o'clock, I could not help it anymore and walked over to Bingyang's house. He had gone to town and was not at home, but I found his wife who greeted me in a friendly way and told me that Yunqian was sick.

"She was quite all right yesterday, and very lively," I said.

"You must have scared her with something," she said. "When she came back home yesterday, she was in very low spirits. She ran into her room and cried, and did not even eat."

"I didn't do anything," I said. "It couldn't be that I didn't ask her to stay for lunch, no?"

"Impossible," Bingyang's wife said. And then, as if pitying me, she said, "That girl doesn't know when something good is happening to her. You indulge her and she'll come up with something. Best to ignore her."

"That can't be it," I said. "Surely there must be a reason."

"Do you want to know the reason?" she laughed.

"Of course."

"It's because you had fowl for lunch yesterday."

I was bewildered. Of course, someone selling turtledoves had come by the previous day. Grandma had asked me whether I liked them and I had said yes. She had bought a couple and that was what I had for lunch.

"Don't be upset," Bingyang's wife said.

"Why would I be upset?"

"People who don't eat meat usually don't care about what others eat," she said, "but Yunqian can't bear to see other people eat meat, especially fowl and poultry. Usually we just won't let her know. That's why we have her eat alone."

"She's a vegetarian?"

"She and her mother always ate vegetarian," she said. "Usually even when she knows that others are eating fowl she never acts like this, but yesterday she cried and cried and did not even have dinner."

"Why didn't Bingyang come over to tell me?"

"Actually, he asked us not to tell you. He said you are teaching her and still she throws a temper because of what you eat;

that's ridiculous. One shouldn't be too kind to that child. If you indulge her, she'll put on an act. With her brother, she's often completely unreasonable."

I thought what she said was extremely unpleasant, but kept quiet. Instead, I got up and asked, "Can I see her?"

"She's in her room." Bingyang's wife got up and led me into an inner room. On a table in front of the window, Yunqian had put her books. There was an old-style bamboo bed and on the right side of the window there were two worn cabinets. On the left, there was an old tea table, and a sheet of paper had been pasted on the wall above. It had Yunqian's handwriting on it. I was stunned: It was my poem "Bird Talk." How deeply she must have felt betrayed by me. I knew that this betrayal was causing her unbearable pain.

Yunqian lay slanted on the bed. She did not show any emotions when we entered, but sat up with her head lowered.

"Yunqian," I said, "why didn't you tell me that you got upset at my mistake? You know, people often make mistakes and don't realize they are wrong unless their parents or teachers point it out to them. It's just like when you make a mistake in arithmetic. You also need someone else to tell you. Nobody is a sage, and we all make mistakes. We might be clever about one thing, but really stupid about another. Haven't I told you that I can be really stupid sometimes? You have to teach me when you know better, just like I teach you things I am good at; isn't that so?"

Yunqian kept her head low and still did not say a word, but from the expression on her face I could see that she was relenting. Bingyang's wife silently looked at Yunqian. She thought that Yunqian had not understood what I had said and hissed sharply, "Here is someone who has come to see you with good intentions and still you are acting like this."

I signaled her to leave it at this and pulled her out with me. Turning my head toward Yunqian, I said, "I'll wait for you tomorrow!"

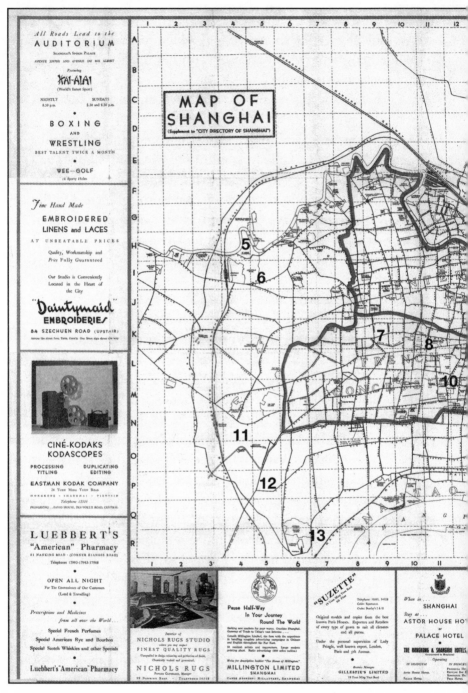

Map of Shanghai from 1932 showing the foreign concessions and larger city area. Numbers refer to locations mentioned in the Introduction and the stories.

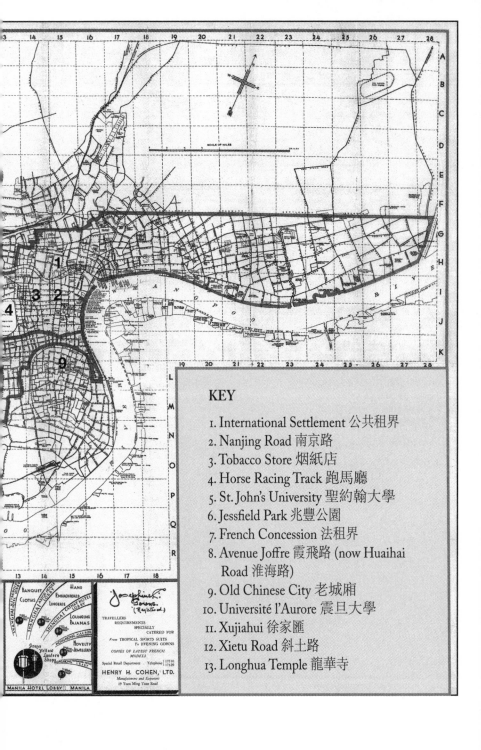

KEY

1. International Settlement 公共租界
2. Nanjing Road 南京路
3. Tobacco Store 烟紙店
4. Horse Racing Track 跑馬廳
5. St. John's University 聖約翰大學
6. Jessfield Park 兆豐公園
7. French Concession 法租界
8. Avenue Joffre 霞飛路 (now Huaihai Road 淮海路)
9. Old Chinese City 老城廂
10. Université l'Aurore 震旦大學
11. Xujiahui 徐家匯
12. Xietu Road 斜土路
13. Longhua Temple 龍華寺

姓名　徐訏
年歲　三十六
職業　掃蕩報記者
籍貫　浙江慈谿
身量
特徵

Xu Xu's self-portrait from 1951.

Detail from Xu Xu's wartime passport that was issued in December 1943 for travel to the US on behalf of the wartime newspaper *Eradicator Daily* 掃蕩報.

Xu Xu in the early 1950s, shortly after arriving in Hong Kong.

Xu Xu lecturing in the 1960s.

Xu Xu with Lin Yutang 林語堂 in Taipei in 1974.

Xu Xu in his home in Hong Kong in the late 1970s.

Cover (*right*) and contents page (*above*) of the bimonthly *Celestial Winds* 宇宙風 from January 1937 that carried Xu Xu's short story "Ghost Love." The cartoon is by Feng Zikai 豐子愷.

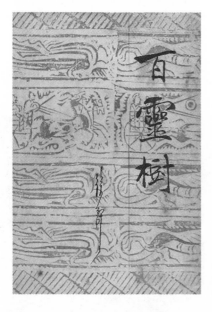

Cover of the anthology *The All-Souls Tree* 百靈樹 from 1951. Xu Xu frequently designed his own book covers.

Cover of volume 1 of *The Complete Works of Xu Xu* 徐訏全集, published in 15 volumes in Taipei by Zhengzhong shuju in 1966. This volume contains the wartime epic *The Rustling Wind* 風蕭蕭.

Cover of the anthology *Step by Step, Mr. Everyman* 小人物的上進 from 1964.

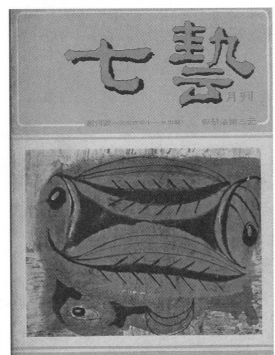

Cover of the monthly *The Seven Arts* 七藝 that Xu Xu started in Hong Kong in 1975.

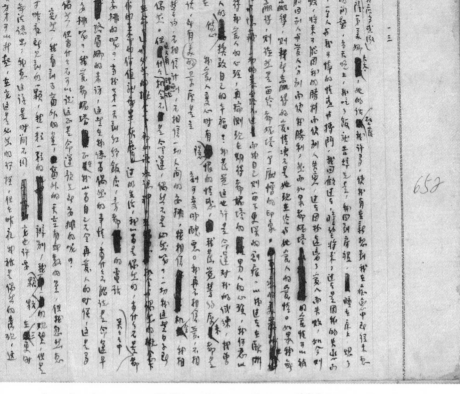

A page from the manuscript of Xu Xu's novel *Time and Brightness* 時與光 from 1966. The number in the right-hand margin is the character count, presumably added by the editor to calculate remuneration.

Movie poster of *Rear Entrance* 後門 (1960), directed by Richard Li Han-hsiang 李翰祥.

Movie still of Xu Xu in his cameo appearance in *Blind Love* 盲戀.

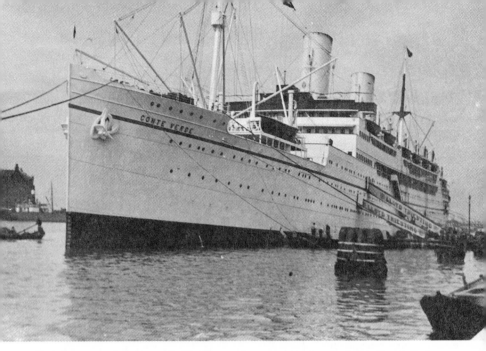

The Italian steamer *Conte Verde* of the Lloyd Triestino line moored pierside at the docks in Shanghai in the late 1930s.

Xu Xu (center) with the cast of *Blind Love* 盲戀 in 1955. Lo Wei 羅維 and Li Li-hua 李麗華 are third from left and right respectively in bottom row. Left to Xu Xu in top row are Peter Chen Ho 陳厚, Evan Yang 易文, who directed the movie, and Kuang Chao Chiang 蔣光超. Pin Ho 賀賓 is second on right of top row, Chung Ching 鍾情 is on the right of bottom row. Next to her is Lai Wang 王萊, who did not star in *Blind Love*.

XI

I could not easily fall asleep that night and lay awake until the early hours. I was awoken by the sound of birds and went into the garden. I saw Yunqian on the other side of the fence, chirping and trilling with the birds. Bathed in sunlight, with that graceful demeanor of hers, her mysterious expression and joyful smile, she seemed like an otherworldly creature. I thought of my vulgar stupidity of eating bird meat. How cruel and repulsive! I felt an unspeakable sense of shame and guilt. I walked through the gate but waited for the birds to fly away and for Yunqian to wave them off before I approached her. In that moment, I noticed in her beautiful appearance a sublime serenity and nobility. Since I had gotten to know her, I had never thought of her as less intelligent or in any way inferior to others, but maybe because I was older than her and had more book knowledge, I had always thought of her as a child. Yet on that day, amidst my own sense of shame and inferiority, did I realize what a pure, unblemished soul she really was.

"Yunqian, I felt bad all last night. I am such a stupid and vulgar person. Thank you for your guidance," I said.

"And I am grateful that you are not upset with me," she said as she greeted me.

"I am the one who needs to thank you," I said. "If it wasn't for you, I would have stayed stupid all my life."

"But I shouldn't have gotten upset, right?"

"No, no, you must have been frightened by me," I said.

"It was just because you said that your heart is that of a bird."

"And yet my mind is that of a wild beast!" I said. "Do you think those birds that just flew off will forgive me?" She fell silent and nodded her head as tears welled up in her eyes. I took her hand and went on a walk with her. Neither of us said a word. The sun shone down on us. As we walked along the rice paddies, the long stalks brushed against our bodies. The hills lay peacefully in the distance, and the nearby woods were lush green. Suddenly, a deep *cucurucucu* drifted over. It was the cry of a turtledove. It was the meat of their kin that I had devoured the day before yesterday. Was this the lament for the dead? Or was it a rebuke for me?

Overcome with sadness, I asked Yunqian, "Did you hear that sound?"

She nodded her head and feeling my heartache said, "They can't know."

I did not utter another word. Holding on to her hand, I walked back with her.

From that day, I began to eat a vegetarian diet. And even though during my years of aimless roaming later in life I resumed eating meat, I never again touched fowl or poultry.

After we had gotten back from our walk, we ate breakfast. At ten thirty, she came back for class. It seemed as if we had grown even closer. Our hearts and minds were in complete union, and I cannot describe the happiness we experienced in each other's company. The weather had started to get hot. The first rice harvest had been brought in, and purple and yellow wildflowers littered the countryside. The sky seemed even clearer now. I had completely recovered, and grandma was convinced that it was thanks to her care while my mother and my friends in the city were convinced that it was my doctor's prescriptions. No one but me knew that it was all thanks to the time I had been able to spend with Yunqian.

I had to start to think about my return to Shanghai. At that time, I was an editor at a newspaper. When I had requested my medical leave, I had asked a friend to replace me temporarily. When he heard that I had recovered, he wrote me a letter, wanting me to come back. But how could I leave Yunqian? And would it not be equally tragic for Yunqian if she were separated from me? I discussed the question of Yunqian attending school in Shanghai with Bingyang. I told him that there were only my mother and me in our house now and that Yunqian could live with us. I guaranteed him that I would look after her like a younger sister and that I would make sure she graduated. I also told him that if he worried about the expense, I would take care of it. Bingyang listened calmly. Finally he said, "Of course I trust you." He paused for a long time, and then asked, "Do you think that is what's best for her?"

"She is the right age to continue her schooling," I said. "Besides, let me tell you that she is just as smart as you are. It's just that your personalities are quite different."

"Maybe," he said, "but no matter, what she needs most is a husband who loves her and can protect her."

I was bewildered by what he had said. Was I not in love with Yunqian? The question had never occurred to me. Now that I thought about it, I realized that there was no denying that I loved her, that I had been in love with her for a long time. I took all my courage and solemnly admitted to Bingyang that I loved her.

"So why don't you marry her?" He asked.

I did not know. Since it had never occurred to me that I had fallen in love with her, I had never thought about marrying her.

I did not have a reply to Bingyang's question. Instead I said, "She is still young. She has no way of knowing whether she loves me, too. She is so pure and innocent and her character is still developing. And it's the first time she has met a man who treats her with respect, isn't it? If she feels that she loves me too," I said, "I will immediately marry her. But, Bingyang, for the sake of her happiness, let her come to Shanghai with me to attend school for one year. We'll return next summer and make a decision. During this one year, I will look after her as if she were my younger sister, you can rest assured of that. And hopefully within the span of one year, she will know whether she wants to be with me, whether she loves me."

Bingyang listened to my confession in silence. Eventually

he said, "Have you asked Yunqian whether she actually wants to go to school in Shanghai?"

"Not yet," I said. "I haven't even dared telling her that I am going back to Shanghai. I've pondered over this for a long time, and felt it was more appropriate to talk to you first. If she had been willing, but you had objected, that would have really broken her heart."

Bingyang again fell silent until he finally got up and said, "She was my mother's favorite child. She might be a little slow, but she is kindhearted and has a beautiful and pure soul. If she decides that she really loves you, I hope you will never fail her." He stood up and got ready to leave. Turning his head, he said, "I will ask her myself tonight."

XII

The reason I had wanted to talk to Bingyang first was that I had already made up my mind that, had he not given his assent, I would have quit my job and stayed with grandma for the time being. But since he had given his blessing and Yunqian had also happily agreed to come to Shanghai for school, I made arrangements to soon return to Shanghai. Naturally, I first wrote to my mother to let her know.

In Shanghai, we lived in a terraced house in the Huaiming-cun neighborhood. It was not a big house, but it was comfortable and quite elegant. My mother lived on the third floor and I lived on the second. Originally, my younger sister had lived in a small back room on the second floor, but the year before she had married a doctor ten years her senior, and soon after they had gone to England. After my sister had gotten married, my mother had felt rather lonely. Fortunately, I still had three older sisters. They were all married, but still lived in Shanghai and often came to our place to see my mother. As for me, except for sleeping and occasionally entertaining friends, I was rarely at home. If Yunqian came to stay with us, she could take my younger sister's place, since her room was empty anyway. This arrangement would also delight my mother.

Everything went well at first. But things began to change when, after a few days, my older sisters came for a visit. Yunqian was not good at socializing and just like back in her village did not know how to please others. She did not like small talk, she could not play cards, and she was not able to help with household chores. What was even more perplexing was that she did not like to walk around the city, go shopping, or immerse herself in the latest fashions. After we first arrived in Shanghai, I wanted to take her to the theater and the movies. We would go together with my mother and sisters, but after a couple of times she asked whether it was all right if she no longer came along. Of course, I said yes. From then on, she never again accompanied us.

I got busy with work, and on top there were all the social obligations one has in a big city. I no longer could spend much time with Yunqian. Yunqian could not get used to mother's lifestyle, and when friends and family visited, she always felt awkward. She soon became very lonely and would not talk with anyone practically all day. When our servants saw that my mother did not like her, they also began to treat her badly and say nasty things about her to my mother. Yunqian never once mentioned any of this to me. I was out all day and often only came home late at night. Without fail, Yunqian would wait up for me. It was only during those hours that I could spend time with her. We would sit for a while in the drawing room and chat a little while having some fruits or snacks I had brought home. She never spoke to me about what happened during the day, and I paid very little attention. In this way, the days passed.

When the new school year was about to begin and schools started to accept applications, I signed her up for two middle schools, but I did not have time to prepare her for the entrance exams. When I accompanied her on the day of the exams, I could see how frightened she was. She did not get into either of the two schools. I read the announcements of the exam results in the newspaper and, realizing how much I had neglected her, rushed home. I found her alone in her room, crying. When she saw me come in, she tried to hide her tears. I told her not to be sad and that I would find her a girls cram school where she could make up her studies. I stayed with her the whole day. In the afternoon, I took her to *Jessfield Park in the International Settlement. I had kept her away from birds all this time, yet when I saw her chirp with the birds in the trees, her face again displayed that bright radiance. We went to the zoo afterward where she happily stood in front of the big cages that held myriad birds. Again and again, she talked about what it must be like to live life in a cage, but after chirping with the caged birds, she no longer seemed to feel particularly uneasy about it. We stayed for a long time and then went to have dinner at a very good vegetarian restaurant. It was quite late when we got home.

The next day, I found her a private tutoring school. I also bought her two caged birds, a thrush and a lark. Those two birds brought her much joy, but after two days, she wanted to set them free. I told her that this was not the right environment. Even if she were to set them free in the park, they probably no longer possessed the ability to look after themselves and that some-one else would catch them. In this world, I told her, there was not another person who loved birds as much as she did, and she should be the one looking after them. I also told her that she could let them out of their cages in her room whenever she wanted to. She accepted my suggestion, and from then on, she had two companions. Whenever I looked at her, she seemed rel-atively happy. She often spoke to me about the two birds, and when I came home in the evening, she wanted me to come into her room and see them. Once she suddenly said to me, "Before I had them, I only lived for that moment when you come home at night. But now, I have two more friends." After I had retired to my room that day, I thought about what she had said and realized how lonely and isolated she was in our house. I gradually noticed how my mother and our servants disdained her and that she was slighted by my friends and family. All of this seemed to have gotten even worse after she had failed to get into school. My only hope now was that she would be a little happier once she started her classes. I also made sure that she would no longer take her lunches at home with my mother.

But only three days after she had taken up classes, she waited for me by the door. I had come home late and everyone else was already asleep. As she walked with me into the drawing room, she said, "I don't want to go to school anymore."

"But why not?" I asked.

"It's just, I feel …"

"Come on now," I said, "you didn't get into middle school, but I found you another school. Give it some time, and you will get used to it. It will be good for you to mix with other people. You can't just …"

She lowered her head and sobbed silently. Finally she stammered, "Let me be your maid. I can serve you. Just don't make me go to school anymore."

"What's all this talk," I said to her. "You are young, and you can learn anything. You must listen to me: You are no different from anyone else! I trust in you and I believe in you, and so does your brother. You don't want to disappoint the two people who have placed so much confidence in you, do you?"

She never once brought this up again. She went to school every day, and when I returned home at night, she would always greet me with a book in hand as she opened the door for me. Whenever I looked at her, she gave me what looked like a happy smile, yet the sparkling radiance gradually disappeared from her eyes.

And then, about a week later, something terrifying happened.

XIII

That evening, I came home around ten. Already from the outside I could hear my mother's loud voice as she was speaking to the servants in the kitchen.

"Who cares whether she wants to eat or not? So my cat killed her birds, but it's not that someone gave the order.... We treat her like a guest, are considerate with her, but she ..."

I hurried inside and ran into my mother, who gave me an account of what had happened. I tried to calm her down and said, "Mother, she is like a small child, don't treat her like an adult." Then I rushed upstairs and went into Yunqian's room. Tears were streaming down her face as she was staring at the two dead birds and the two empty cages. Her cheeks that had seemed like white porcelain the first time I had seen her seemed even whiter and paler now. She was trembling, both because of her grief for her two dead friends and because she feared my mother's anger. When she saw me, she pulled me close to her tear-stricken face and sobbed, "I let you down, I am sorry!"

"No, it's my fault, it's all my fault." I held her face in my hands, unable to withhold my own tears. She fell silent and just gazed at me blankly. She was still trembling, and her white cheeks, like frost-covered water lilies, were icy cold. Her lips were quivering and her eyes were flickering like stars in a frosty sky. The bleak whiteness of her countenance resembled a plum blossom in the snow, revealing the purity and nobility, the modesty and holiness of her soul. I bent down to her, clasping her frigid hands, pressing my face against hers.

"Let me go home tomorrow, please," she whispered.

"Of course ... but I will go with you," I replied, kneeling in front of her, kissing her hands.

She fell silent again. When she lifted her head, I asked, "Will you marry me? And live with me elsewhere?"

"Are you sure you want me?" She asked.

"I am just afraid I am not worthy of you," I replied.

"I am not worthy. I know I am not worthy," she said, gazing at me blankly. "You have your work, your friends, your social circle; you have a future, and I don't have anything to offer."

"But I love you. Without you, I am nothing."

"I will be yours forever, I will always be yours," she said, "but you should think carefully. I am a dimwit. I can't study, I can't socialize, I can't get anything done. I am unworthy of your love and I am unfit for this world."

Noticing that I hadn't left Yunqian's room all this time, my mother started to make a fuss again. Yunqian told me to go downstairs, but I did not listen. We held each other tight and did not speak. After some time, I heard my mother angrily leave the house. I said, "Let's go to Hangzhou tomorrow and stay there for a while. The aunt of a friend of mine runs a convent. She rents out rooms. I have stayed there before. She is a widow and does not have any children. That's why she set up a convent and practices Buddhism. The place is very quiet and peaceful. Once we get there we can plan our further steps. Life in Shanghai is too chaotic anyway. Hangzhou is much more quiet. If I can find work in Hangzhou, we might as well live there. What do you think?"

"You know that I don't understand these things," she said, still trembling. "I trust you. Let's do what you think is best." Engulfed by the night, we lay silently in close embrace, listening to each other's heart beat as the hours passed. I finally urged her to go to sleep and told her to pack her belongings the next morning. Only then did I retire to my room.

I left the house early the next day. I withdrew some money, asked for another leave from my newspaper, and found someone who could replace me. I told my mother that I would accompany Yunqian home and then boarded the ten-past-one train to Hangzhou with her. The journey took us through lush, green plains flanked by hills and rivers, and Yunqian glowed like a bird that had been let out of a cage and returned to the forest. Her face shone like a small white cloud in the sun.

XIV

The Buddhist name of my friend's aunt was Pengwu. She was skilled in traditional painting and poetry and, after her husband's early death, had devoted herself to Buddhism, studying under a learned, old nun called Master Fazang. Sister Pengwu had not actually taken the vows but had set up Baojue Convent and lived there with Master Fazang who, despite her seventy-six years, was still hale and hearty. Master Fazang did not involve herself in the day-to-day running of the convent and rarely left her room.

Baojue Convent was not very big. The principal compound was made up of three parts: a main hall and an eastern and a western wing, each of which had three rooms. The kitchen was located at the end of the eastern wing, and behind the western wing there was another small courtyard with two more small buildings that were sometimes rented out to worshippers. In the back of the main hall there was a bamboo garden, and in the courtyard in front there were two stone stelae shaped like lotus flowers and an incense burner made of cast iron. The main gate was on the left, and on the right was a bed of lush green nandina shrubs. Sister Pengwu put me up in one of the small buildings in the adjacent courtyard and Yunqian in one of the wing rooms of the main courtyard next to Master Fazang. It was already late when we arrived and, after a snack and a little chat with Sister Pengwu, we soon went to bed.

I got up early the next morning. I walked over to the main courtyard where I saw Yunqian listening to the birds. Grains of rice had been sprinkled at the base of the stone stelae as bird feed. A swarm of sparrows flew over from the eaves of the temple roof to the stone stelae, and then from the stone stelae to the bed of nandinas. Nobody had ever frightened them here or done them any harm, and they flew about freely. Yunqian seemed to have entered a world of her own. She was smiling as she was talking to the birds in a low voice, and her face glowed with that same mysterious radiance. Soon she was encircled by the sparrows, a sight that caused wonder among Sister Pengwu and two or three of the younger nuns. Yunqian all the while did not notice me, and only when Sister Pengwu called out to her did we have our breakfast.

After breakfast, Yunqian and I went for a walk. Baojue Convent was located on a hillside and we walked up the slope. We passed through a dense bamboo thicket until we reached a pavilion. Only then did we go back. In the afternoon I took a nap, and when I got up, I noticed that Yunqian and Sister Pengwu were talking and laughing together like old acquaintances. I was quite surprised at this as Yunqian did not usually warm up to people easily and did not let people get close to her either, yet it seemed different with Sister Pengwu. I started to wonder if maybe this was what people referred to as fate. Sister Pengwu could not possibly have understood Yunqian right away, and why should Yunqian have felt differently about the convent than about our home in Shanghai? Yet the way she behaved around Sister Pengwu and the others in the convent was so different from the way she had behaved around my mother and my friends and relatives. Here, she was her lively, natural self and found it easy to talk to people. It was as if she had lived here for a long time already. But things took an even stranger turn from here.

In the morning of the third day, when the two of us had left for a walk, Yunqian suddenly said, "I think Master Fazang really likes me. Last night she taught me the Heart Sutra."

"Master Fazang?" I was amazed, because I knew that Master Fazang only very rarely left her study. When she did, she would smile at people and murmur a few Buddhist "amituofo" blessings, but she never said much else.

"She asked me to come to her room," Yunqian said.

"Did you like the Heart Sutra?" I asked.

"Yes," she said, her face shining with a marvelous radiance. "I can already recite it from memory. It's even more interesting than poetry."

"You can already recite it from memory?" I asked in surprise.

"How about I'll recite it for you?" And she began to recite fluently. Her low murmur again was imbued with a marvelous beauty.

I was in awe. I silently walked behind her as we followed a rivulet downstream. It was a little cloudy, and the sun would hide and then reappear. Down below in the plain, there were rice paddies and the cooking smoke from farmhouses hung in the air. We were now surrounded by trees, and from time to time we could hear birds singing. Yunqian and I were the only ones in this tranquil world.

When she finished her recital, she abruptly said: "Do you see that kingfisher in the tree? It's so beautiful."

And sure enough, high up in a tree I saw a bluish-green bird with a long tail. It seemed that Yunqian was murmuring something to the bird and then she said, "Let's go back."

"Are you tired?" I asked.

"No," she said, "Sister Pengwu lent me a copy of the Diamond Sutra. Maybe you can teach it to me today?"

"I am not sure I understand all of it," I replied.

"It's strange," she said, "I like it, and it doesn't seem hard to understand."

When we returned to the convent, we sat down at a table in the back courtyard and I interpreted the Diamond Sutra for her sentence by sentence. Her eyes glowed with a mysterious radiance. She was fascinated, and whenever we came across a passage that was hard for me to explain, she would just say, "Don't worry, don't worry; keep going!" We labored on all morning and afternoon, but what a peaceful and harmonious day we had!

On the fourth day, I went to look up some friends. Yunqian did not accompany me and stayed behind in the convent. My plan was to first find a job and then find a house in a quiet location that was still close enough to my work. Once everything was settled, we would get married. I had made up my mind that, for her sake, we would lead a simple and quiet life, without the kind of socializing she so abhorred; in harmony with nature; and in close proximity to mountains and rivers, forests and birds. But these were all things that I had contemplated while lying awake at night or after waking up in the early hours before dawn. I had never discussed them with Yunqian. After we had arrived at Baojue Convent, Yunqian had been just as calm and happy as she had been back home, spending all day in the company of birds. There was a peaceful smile on her face, and her eyes shone marvelously. I had not wanted to bother her, because I knew that with her childlike character, she had no judgment of such practical matters. Besides, she had complete faith in me. But now I had to tell her. I would tell her the moment I got back to the convent, because I was just too excited and happy. I must have sung and screamed all the way up the hill until I reached Baojue Convent.

Sister Pengwu was conducting the evening recitation and Yunqian was waiting for me in the courtyard. I embraced her as soon as I had entered. I then told her that I had paid visits to three friends, and that I had been really lucky. One of my friends worked in a library, and he had told me that they were looking for a new director. Another friend was the director of a middle school, and he had told me that they were short of an English teacher. They both would be thrilled if I were to accept the position. The third one worked for a newspaper, and he had told me that he could take me on immediately. Originally, I had worried about not being able to find work, and now there were three jobs to choose from. I then told her all my plans for us. I said that I would make a decision about which position to accept tonight, and then would go and look for a house for us to live in. Once I had found a suitable house and it had been fixed up, I would show it to her. Then we could get married and go on a trip to visit the hills and lakes of the lower Yangtze region for a couple of weeks before I took up my new post.

I took her arm as we stood by the main gate, gazing at the setting sun. Cooking smoke from farmhouses drifted in the valley below, and the ravens returned home to the forest. I poured my heart out to her and declared my love to her. I told her that I had made up my mind to leave behind my meaningless life in the city and to live a simple and peaceful life with her in the countryside. Yunqian, however, remained silent. I looked at her. The evening sun shone on her beautiful cheeks, making them look like petals of a lotus flower. The pureness of her face was heightened by the faint smile she wore. Without looking at me, she took out two pieces of paper that had divination rhymes written on them. She gave me one, and said, "This one is for you."

I took it and looked at it. It read:

There is a cause for everything if long enough thou ponder.
A worldly man in brocade robes can never with immortals wander.

I was overcome by an indescribable emotion. I read the prophecy over and over. Then Yunqian passed me the other slip and said, "This one is mine."

I took it and read:

Fear not that enlightenment will never come near
For with the right karma you might find it at dawn.
The heart of the jade goddess is pure and clear,
Her senses are empty and her wisdom will spawn.

I was speechless. I silently gazed at the last rays of the setting sun. In that moment, neither reason nor my knowledge of science could tame that strange superstitious belief that was taking hold of me. And what if it was superstition! There was a sublime beauty to it.

After a long silence, Yunqian said, "This place has become heaven for me."

I still was not able to say anything.

"Master Fazang and Sister Pengwu don't take me for the dimwit others think I am, and they know I am not stupid."

"But I ..."

"You are a good person, but when I am with you, I feel that I am burdening you. When I am with them, I feel that I am helping them."

I did not understand. But what did I ever understand?

I turned around and walked into the convent. I began to hate Master Fazang. What magic had this old nun used to bewitch Yunqian? Alone, without Yunqian, I went into Master Fazang's room. The light had not been turned on, and it was dim inside. Master Fazang was holding a string of prayer beads and was reciting sutras, eyes closed. Without opening her eyes she said, "Please sit down."

She smiled at me, her wrinkled face full of kindness and humor. Her smile had a calming effect on me. I sat for a long time, mulling over the words I had wanted to say to her, but was unable to say anything. Finally I opened my mouth.

"Master Fazang, do you really think this is the right place for Yunqian?"

"Who but herself would know the answer?"

I didn't reply.

"What use is there for us to interpret as suffering what she thinks is happiness?"

There wasn't anything left for me to say. I sat stiffly for a long while. The sky grew gradually darker, and when it was pitch black in the room, I got up and said, "I thank you."

XV

I tossed and turned all night. The next morning I got up while the morning recitation was taking place. In front of the main hall, I saw Yunqian already dressed in a nun's robe, assisting Sister Pengwu with the ceremony.

After breakfast, when I was alone in my room, Sister Pengwu came in to see me.

"Yunqian is still willing to do whatever you think is best," she said. 'If you really feel that … you know she feels terrible about it all."

"I know."

"Yet she was destined to be here."

"I believe so."

"She can stay here for a while and doesn't have to be ordained right away. She is already a vegetarian," Sister Pengwu said. "If you work in Hangzhou, you can come as often as you please. That wouldn't be too bad, would it? Getting married and starting a family, would that really mean happiness to the both of you? You are an intelligent person. You know her much better than I do and her happiness surely is of even greater concern to you than it is to me. You decide."

I thanked her, and she left. Alone again, I sank into a deep state of contemplation. If I were to listen to Sister Pengwu's advice, work in Hangzhou, and come here every week to see Yunqian; maybe that would be a happy life? But I knew I could not do it. I could not rid myself of my earthly desires. I did not want to be selfish, but still I couldn't help it. I knew well that Yunqian was detached from such yearnings and that she was of a nobler kind. She did not belong with me; she belonged in a world unspoiled by worldly matters. Only in such a world could her sublimity and magnificence manifest itself. Only in such a world could she truly feel at ease and be happy. I would be of no help or value to her. I had become superfluous. In fact, I had become an emotional burden to her, just like she had been a burden to me in Shanghai. What was there left to say? I did not see Yunqian again. Early the next day, I descended the hill and immediately returned to Shanghai.

My life in Shanghai returned to its usual grind. Petty quarrels and social engagements kept me busy, and I had my share of ups and downs. I was hoping that I would quickly forget Yunqian, yet she would invariably appear in my mind in moments of fatigue and loneliness, even though our worlds were so far apart. After two months, Bingyang suddenly came to see me. He told me that he had received a letter from Yunqian. He had written a reply, urging her to get married to me, but she wrote back telling him that Baojue Convent was like heaven to her and that she wanted to stay there. Worried at first, he had made a trip to the convent to see for himself. He had stayed there for a week, but when he saw how happy Yunqian was and how she talked and laughed with the other nuns, his mind was put at rest. Before he left, he made a donation to the convent as a token of support for his sister. And that was the last news I had of Yunqian.

In the years that followed, I wandered aimlessly. I indulged in wine and women, and I got worn down by poverty and sickness, living out of tiny rooms. I threw myself into frivolous affairs and participated in noisy brawls. I changed from one job to the next and drifted from place to place. I married, got divorced, raised kids, went to America, Europe, and Africa. I sold my songs and my stories and everything else to make ends meet. And in the end, I drifted to Hong Kong.

I forgot Yunqian. I forgot her a long time ago, but every time I travel to the countryside and gaze at the mountains and streams and the lush forests, and I hear the distant singing of birds, the figure of Yunqian faintly flashes into my memory. But it is just like a fleecy cloud drifting by in the sky, and as soon as I return to my mundane existence, I forget her again. How many times had I thought of writing her a letter to ask how she was doing; but when I looked at my own vulgar life, I could never muster the courage to disturb her pure and peaceful soul. Once, five years ago, after I had returned from abroad, I wrote a letter to Bingyang, but I did not receive a reply.

Yet when I received the Diamond Sutra through the mail, I realized at once that it was the one that Master Fazang had lent Yunqian and that we had studied together on our third day in Baojue Convent, sitting at the table in the small courtyard. The letter and the sutra had been sent from my grandmother's village. I did not know which of my relatives still lived there or how they had gotten hold of my address. That of course was not too difficult, since many of my relatives and friends in Shanghai knew of my whereabouts. In any case, I had no desire to know. I looked at myself in the mirror. What a vulgar face! I had long stopped being a vegetarian, even if I still did not touch poultry or fowl. I tossed away the mirror. As my tears fell on the open sutra, my eyes caught sight of a line in the opening chapter:

> All sentient beings, whether born from eggs or born from a womb or born from moisture or born through metamorphosis, whether born with physical form or without, be they capable of reason or incapable of reason or neither capable nor incapable or reason, all will eventually be led by me to enter Nirvana where all their anguish will be extinguished.

百靈樹
The All-Souls Tree

"The All-Souls Tree," published in Hong Kong in 1950, is another short story that explores the theme of exile. The story is set in Taiwan after the Nationalists' retreat to the island in the wake of their defeat by Communist forces during the civil war. Taiwan had been a Japanese colony from 1895 until the end of World War II, when sovereignty over the island was transferred to Chiang Kai-shek's Nationalist government. By the end of 1949, large parts of the Nationalist government as well as approximately two million troops along with their families and other civilians had arrived there from the mainland.

The short story recounts a mystifying incident that occurs when a group of friends undertake a trip to *Mount Ali 阿里山, one of Taiwan's most scenic tourist destinations. The friends take a train from the capital Taipei 台北 in the north to *Chiayi 嘉義, a town in central Taiwan. From there, they board a famous *narrow-gauge railway to the top of Mount Ali that had originally been built to transport timber down the mountain. During the colonial period, the Japanese had developed the island's infrastructure, in large part to facilitate the transport of agricultural produce and the extraction of natural resources. In addition, many Japanese-style buildings, like the hotel the group is staying in on Mount Ali, were erected during colonial rule and continued to be used thereafter.

Throughout the narrative, there are several references to *Beiping, which was the official name of Beijing during the Republican period after Chiang Kai-shek had moved the capital to Nanjing in 1927. In defiance of

Mao Zedong moving the capital back to Beijing in 1949, the name Beiping continued to be used in Taiwan until the 1980s. The story's female protagonist also mentions that the bank for which she works had recently been transferred to Taiwan. Many important financial institutions were relocated to Taiwan as the Nationalists' military defeat on the mainland became more likely.

Strange Tales from a Chinese Studio 聊齋志異, also cited in "Ghost Love," is a well-known eighteenth-century collection of ghost stories. Toward the end of the story, the narrator makes a reference to Lin Daiyu 林黛玉, the tragic heroine of the famous eighteenth-century novel *Dream of the Red Chamber* 紅樓夢 who died from a broken heart upon learning that her cousin Jia Baoyu 賈寶玉 would marry his other cousin Xue Baochai 薛寶釵 instead of her.

Mr. Wang was a conscientious man who did not lack a sense of humor. Besides, he was calm and composed in all his dealings with others. He had to go to *Chiayi to take care of some business related to his factory, and his son Dawen was going with him to visit the campus of a college at Taichung. Mr. Wang knew that I had often spoken of taking a trip to *Mount Ali, and, because Mount Ali is not far from Chiayi, he invited us to come along. We all knew that he had friends down south and that he knew his way around. Finding accommodation and organizing transportation would all be easy. Everyone was excited. There were going to be seven of us: Ms. Nie, Ms. Li, Xianmeng and his wife Cunmei, Mr. Wang and his son, and me. But then, shortly before the trip, Xianmeng announced that his cousin Xiancheng was able to come along as well, because the trip happened to fall on a bank holiday. And so we bought eight train tickets.

Everyone knew each other well, with the exception of Xianmeng's cousin Xiancheng. Other than Xianmeng and his wife, only I was acquainted with her, having met her several times at Xianmeng's house. She was a rather unusual girl. Her appearance was unusual, her manner was unusual, even her character was somewhat unusual. She was not tall, but she looked rather tall, because her body was well proportioned. Her facial features were not exactly beautiful. She had a low hairline. Her forehead protruded a little and her lower jaw was pointed, but luckily her cheekbones were not too high and her cheeks bore soft curves. Her chin was round and resembled a little fruit, and her nose was upright. She had big eyes whose corners were slightly curved upward. Her eyebrows were nicely shaped and well balanced. They were very delicate and very enticing. Yet she did not apply any makeup and dressed like a middle school student.

The first time I met her was shortly after the lunar New Year. Xianmeng was entertaining a lot of guests that day, and everyone was playing dominoes. Xiancheng at first joined in the fun and stood by the table to place some bets, but then, all of a sudden, without having either lost or won much money, she suddenly withdrew to a sofa in the corner of the room and began to knit. I wanted to go over and to talk to her but felt a little awkward because we were not properly acquainted. A few days later, I ran into Xianmeng's wife Cunmei and I asked whether Xiancheng often came to their house.

"She's a little odd," Cunmei said. "Sometimes she does, but then we suddenly won't see her for months. Sometimes when she is supposed to come for dinner, she won't even show up."

"Is she at school?" I asked.

"No, she works at a bank," Cunmei said.

"Does she live in a company dorm?"

"No," Cunmei answered. "Sometimes she lives with us, and then on a whim she suddenly moves in with Xianmeng's elder brother. At first I thought it was me she had a problem with, but later I realized that's just the way she is. When she feels like it, she'll suddenly move in with us again. That's why I don't try to keep her when she leaves, and don't turn her away when she comes back."

"How odd," I said.

"Yes, she's a little odd. I don't really understand her," Cunmei replied. "You would think that a twenty-two- or twenty-three-year-old girl would enjoy dressing up, but she doesn't like it at all. It's not that her salary is too low, either. She doesn't even have to pay for food or lodging. But still, she never has any clothes made for her."

"But that day when I saw her, wasn't she dressed really nicely?"

"Oh, that striped, woolen *qipao*? I gave that to her," Cunmei said. "During the first month after the Lunar New Year, we always host a lot of guests. Xiancheng is Xianmei's cousin, and now she lives with us. What do you think people would say if they saw her wear the same simple, blue-cotton dress every day? They would think that I …"

Cunmei was a clever and capable woman. Appearance mattered a great deal to her, and she was very ambitious. She expected her maids to be tidy and neatly dressed and naturally did not want her cousin to be careless about her outfit. But sure enough, the next few times I ran into Xiancheng, she was always dressed extremely plainly. But this did not diminish the natural charm of her youthful appearance. On the contrary, it only made me more aware of it. Her eyes always sparkled with a radiant intelligence. I enjoyed talking to her and she likewise seemed happy when I did. At first, she always seemed a little shy, yet her replies would be very sophisticated. But then, she would often suddenly excuse herself for no apparent reason and walk away from the conversation. After that, even though I was a frequent visitor to Xianmeng's house, I no longer ran into her. I assumed that she must have moved in with Xianmeng's brother and that she probably would not be back for a while. And so it was a bit of a surprise that she was going to travel to Mount Ali with us.

Mount Ali is covered in virgin forest. When Taiwan was a Japanese colony, a railway line had been built from Chiayi to the top of the mountain in order to facilitate the logging of timber. Setting out from Taipei, we naturally first had to take a train to Chiayi. Our tickets had all been arranged in advance, and Ms. Nie, Ms. Li, and I went to the station together. We were going to meet up with Mr. Wang and his son as well as Xianmeng, Cunmei, and Xiancheng on the train, and when we boarded, Xianmeng, Cunmei, and Xiancheng were already in their seats. I introduced Xiancheng to Ms. Nie and Ms. Li, and they liked each other right away. Shortly afterward, Mr. Wang and his son Dawen also got on board. Dawen was a sophomore at college, and he was thinking of transferring to a vocational industrial college in Taichung. He wanted to see if the school was a good fit and whether transferring there was an option. He was about twenty-four years old and was healthy looking and energetic. He knew how to drive and was a good swimmer. He could fix a radio and sing English songs, and he played tennis and bridge. Naturally, I also introduced them to Xiancheng. The six of us at first had been sitting together in two rows of seats facing each other. When Mr. Wang and his son came on board, Xiancheng and I got up while Dawen put his father's luggage into the luggage rack. Then Mr. Wang and I went to sit in a pair of seats on the right of the aisle.

We all experience youth at some point, and there invariably is a time when our behavior somewhat resembles that of animals. A rooster likes to crow in front of a hen, a stag during mating season likes to grunt. Once Dawen had laid eyes on Xiancheng, he could not hold back. He would look at her again and again, suddenly start singing, get up and sit down again, stare out of the window, or take out a deck of cards and keep shuffling them. Xiancheng at first had been quite jovial and talkative, but then all of a sudden fell silent, swapped seats with Cunmei, and stared out the window.

The train had left the city behind and open fields were now sweeping past the window. As the train was picking up speed, everyone's conversation slowed to a halt as if lacking the energy to speak. Even Dawen, who was humming an English pop song while still fiddling with his deck of cards, seemed a little lost for words. Eventually, Ms. Li suggested that we play a game of cards. No one objected, yet when she asked Xiancheng, Xiancheng said with a smile, "I don't know how to play."

"I'll teach you!"

Dawen happily rose to his feet, ready to swap seats with Xianmeng, but Xiancheng threw me a glance and calmly said, "Why don't you let Mr. Xu play instead?"

She got up while she spoke and walked in my direction to swap seats with me. Of course I could not decline, and so I took her seat. She remained in that seat all the way to Chiayi.

Mr. Wang had called in advance and so we were met at the station by a friend of his. Chiayi is not a big city. There were only a handful of hotels, and our rooms were quite small. There were two of us to a room. I shared a room with Xianmeng, and Mr. Wang and his son occupied another. Ms. Nie and Ms. Li stayed together in one room and so did Cunmei and Xiancheng. Mr. Wang's friend then treated us to a lavish dinner, and it was already quite late when we returned to the hotel. Since we were going up into the mountains early the next day, we all went to bed right away.

The next morning, we took a diesel-powered train into the mountains. Another friend of Mr. Wang's from Chiayi, a certain Mr. Shi, came with us as well. The scenery along the way was lush. We traversed a tunnel and, shortly thereafter, another one. We climbed to a mountain pass, and once we passed it, we approached another one. It was spring, but after three or four hours, the scenery started to change as if there had been a change of season. The temperature also got colder; we were already inside the clouds. Everybody had been cheerful at first, but then the women among us all got a little tired. Even after they had put on their overcoats they complained that it was still chilly. When it then also started to rain, everyone's laughter and chatter dwindled. Only Dawen was still humming along.

Xiancheng, who was sitting next to me at the time, suddenly leaned toward me and said, "I feel I have seen this landscape somewhere before."

"Mountainscapes always resemble each other a little," I said.

It seemed as if she had not taken note of what I had just said. She remained silent and gazed at the mountains, spellbound. I followed her line of vision to a steep cliff directly facing us. The bottom of the cliff was covered in undergrowth and was sloping toward the ravine. Hundreds of meters down below, one could see the violent currents of a mountain stream. On this side of the stream, the slope was covered by forest, which was crisscrossed by little paths. High above, one could see the meandering rails where our diesel engine was headed. At that time, the mountains were shrouded by a sea of clouds. The sky above was ash-gray. Below, mist was clinging to the slopes, forming thick clouds one moment and then dispersing the next. The whole mountain range looked as if covered by a layer of fine gauze.

"Strange. I am sure I have seen this place in my dreams," Xiancheng suddenly said.

I did not reply but felt that this was a sensation many people experience. We come to a place for the first time, but feel we have seen it in our dreams before. There is a psychological explanation for this. We might have seen a painting of Mount Ali, and in our dreams it then becomes a real landscape. When we then see the actual mountainscape, we think that we have seen it in our dreams.

By the time we reached the mountaintop, it was already late morning. During the colonial period, vacation homes had been built here for wealthy Japanese. Later, those buildings had been turned into hotels, and that was where we had planned to put up for the night. Our hotel was an elegant Japanese-style building. On the second floor, it had a spacious balcony, the front of which was enclosed with large windows from where you could gaze at the mist-shrouded mountain ranges. Far in the distance, you could see the faint outlines of a few snow-covered peaks.

It was quite cold and the hotel staff had brought out a brazier for us. They had also prepared padded cotton kimonos and all of us put one on, but Ms. Nie and Ms. Li were so tired that they immediately lay down on their beds, covering themselves with thick padded blankets. Mr. Wang and his friend Mr. Shi asked the hotel to have our lunch prepared, and I went up to the balcony. Xiancheng was standing by one of the windows, gazing into the distance. The kimono she was wearing made her look even more charming. Suddenly, Dawen also appeared on the balcony, jovially singing a foreign song. He wanted to talk to

Xiancheng, it seemed, and so I went to stand on the other side of the balcony, where I was joined by Xianmeng and Cunmei. Xiancheng only had eyes for what lay in front of the window and had not noticed any of us. Only when Dawen had come up close behind her did she raise her head. She saw the three of us on the other side and, as if to avoid Dawen, walked over to us.

Gazing into the distance from our vantage point, all we could see were mountain ridges amidst a sea of clouds, but closer by, we could see a valley and a number of ragged rocks protruding from high above. Xiancheng suddenly said, "Those rocks look as if they are about to tumble down."

"But they are rooted deep in the ground," Xianmeng said, "and even if a hundred people stood on top of them, they wouldn't budge."

"But those one hundred people might all fall down," Cunmei said jokingly.

"Would you die if you jumped down from there?" Xiancheng asked.

"Even if you didn't die you would still break every bone in your body," I said with a chuckle.

It had been drizzling when we first got to the hotel, but now the drizzle had turned into sleet. By the time we were done with our lunch, it was snowing. Most of us agreed that we should wait for the weather to clear up and then explore the next day, and that today we would just stay at the hotel and play cards. We were all pretty tired and exhausted on account of the previous day's train journey and the uncomfortable night in the small hotel in Chiayi. In the morning, we had gotten up early to catch the train for the journey up the mountain that had taken several hours. Once we had eaten our fill and had warmed up, everyone wanted to take an afternoon nap. I slept for about an hour and a half. When I woke up, I noticed that everyone else was still asleep. It was still snowing, and the hotel felt deserted. I put on the padded kimono and wore my raincoat over it and then went outside to take a walk. It was cold outside, but the snow had let up a little and the wind was not very strong. The sky was still overcast and the mountain ranges kept disappearing and reappearing amidst the clouds. It looked spectacular.

There was a fork in the road ahead of me. One road led up the mountain, the other down. I followed the road going up. I had only walked a few steps when I noticed a woman dressed in a kimono and holding a Japanese umbrella ahead of me. At first I thought it was another hotel guest, but then I recognized the leather shoes and the rim of the dress that showed from under the kimono, and I realized it was Xiancheng. I called out to her and she turned her head. I noticed that she was holding a branch covered in leaves.

"You didn't go to sleep?" I asked.

"I slept a little, but when I got up and saw that you were all still fast asleep, I went out for a walk," she replied.

"Where did you get that umbrella?" I asked, having now caught up with her. "I almost didn't recognize you."

"I borrowed it from the hotel." Walking next to me now, she waved the tree branch she was holding and asked, "Do you know what kind of tree this is?"

"I think I have seen it in other places as well," I said, "but I can't think of the name."

"We have them in my home province too," she said. "In our local dialect they are called 'all-souls trees.' They are said to convey omens. They seem to be smaller here."

"That's probably because of the climate." I said. "But can such a small all-souls tree also convey omens?"

She did not reply. We walked next to each other for a while until I could no longer bear the silence and said, "The others really are healthy sleepers. When I got up, they were all still sound asleep."

We kept walking. Ahead of us, the road began to slope down. Below, there were several Japanese wooden houses. Cooking smoke was already rising from their chimneys. Xiancheng walked to the point where the road began to descend and stopped. Like in a trance she gazed at the mountain range to the left of us that was protruding from a thick sea of clouds. I followed her gaze and marveled at the scene. After a while, the clouds began to stir and a gust of wind caught Xiancheng's umbrella. I quickly helped her close it up and took it from her. The snow had almost stopped.

"Let's go back," I said. "Aren't you cold?" She nodded and we walked back together. After a few dozen steps, we ran into Dawen who had a camera round his neck and came walking toward us, humming a tune. I called out to him.

"So you got up as well?"

"Everyone's up and playing cards," he said. "They asked me to get you."

"We are heading back now," Xiancheng said.

"Let me take a picture of the two of you," Dawen said.

"Is there enough light?" I asked.

"I have a very good lens, f2 aperture," he said, standing by the side of the road and opening the camera case.

"I'd rather not have my photo taken," Xiancheng said with a smile and continued to walk down at an accelerated pace.

"Well, then I can take one of you alone," Dawen said to her, thinking that she did not want her picture taken together with me.

"I've never liked having my picture taken," Xiancheng said, still smiling.

"What's wrong with having one's photo taken?" Dawen asked jokingly. He seemed to think that Xiancheng was just being prudish.

Fearing that he would say something that might displease her, I quickly turned toward Xiancheng and said, "Maybe you can take a photo of me and Dawen?"

She nodded, and Dawen, after having adjusted the lens,

passed the camera to Xiancheng and came over to stand next to me. Xiancheng did not have anywhere to put the branch of the all-souls tree she was still holding, and so she said to me, "This is for you."

I quickly walked a few steps down to her and, taking the branch, asked, "Are you sure you want me to have it?"

She smiled at me. Her eyes suddenly sparkled with a beautiful radiance. Never before or after did she leave such a deep impression on me. I ran back to where Dawen was standing, and Xiancheng took a photo of the two of us. That is why in that photograph I am holding a branch of the all-souls tree. It is the one Xiancheng gave me on that day.

When we returned to the hotel, everyone was playing cards, and we joined in a round of Cheats and Dunners.

After dinner, Mr. Wang's friend Mr. Shi was generous enough to share a can of ground coffee with everyone. As we were enjoying our coffee, Mr. Wang started to tell ghost stories. Each one of us then took turns and told one as well. The more stories we heard, the more scared we became. There was no electric light on the mountain, and it was completely silent outside. The snow and the rain had stopped, it seemed, but from time to time a gust of wind would rattle the windowpanes. I am usually not afraid of ghosts, but even I could not help feeling a little frightened. Mr. Wang, Xianmeng, and Dawen were even more spooked than me, and the women all were cowering against the wall, not daring to move. Only Xiancheng's appearance had not changed, and she was still talking in a calm and composed manner.

"You are not at all scared?" I asked her.

"I don't believe in ghosts," she said with a smile. "But if ghosts do exist, each of us will turn into one after we die, so what's there to be afraid of? And if ghosts don't exist, then there is even less reason to be afraid of them."

"People who are terrified of ghosts don't care whether they exist or not," Xianmeng said. "They are afraid, regardless of whether they exist or not."

"What is that supposed to mean?" Xiancheng asked skeptically.

"I think it's just like when people who are in love long for their lover, and people who don't have a lover nevertheless long for an ideal lover," I said jokingly, wanting to steer the conversation away from ghosts. My comment made everyone laugh, everyone except for Xiancheng, who fell silent.

"The sky has pretty much cleared up," Mr. Wang said. "Tomorrow, everyone should get up early and see the sunrise."

"Well, we should sleep early then," I said.

Mr. Wang then brought up the question of rooming. We had four rooms in total, two upstairs and two downstairs. The upstairs rooms were a little nicer while the downstairs rooms were Japanese-style and one would have to sleep on a tatami mat. It seemed appropriate to let the women sleep upstairs while we men would stay downstairs. However, Ms. Li, Ms. Nie, and Cunmei all were scared of ghosts. They said that if the four of them slept upstairs and something happened, even if they cried out, there would be no one to help them. Ms. Li was the first to object to the arrangement. Then Cunmei, who had studied in Japan and liked to sleep on tatami mats, said that she would prefer to sleep downstairs. In a bed, she added, two people have to squeeze under one blanket, but on a tatami, one can stretch out as one pleases. And so it went back and forth until it was decided that two of the men would stay in one of the upstairs rooms and two of the women in the other. For the downstairs rooms, it was going to be the same.

Ms. Li and Ms. Nie as well as Mr. Shi and Dawen were going to sleep upstairs. Mr. Wang, who was quite portly, preferred to sleep on a tatami instead of having to share a bed and thus shared a downstairs room with me and Xianmeng. Cunmei and Xiancheng shared the other downstairs room. In the end, everybody was happy. Holding flashlights and candles, those of us sleeping downstairs descended the stairs. By that time, it was already past ten.

We entered the rooms from a little porch-like corridor and took off our shoes. The side of the corridor facing outward was made of glass, while the one facing inward consisted of Japanese shōji panels, each made of thin wooden strips in a lattice of equal-size squares pasted over with paper. There were about five or six rooms stretching the length of the corridor, each separated from the next by a set of shōji panels. We let the women sleep in the outermost room while we slept in the room next to them. We did not know whether the room adjacent to us was occupied by another guest. But since it was pitch black inside the rooms, it would not have mattered whether that room was empty. The women would have been scared sleeping next to it no matter what.

The rooms were very clean, and once the three of us had entered ours, each one of us picked a corner and got ready to sleep. I was still chatting with Xianmeng by the time Mr. Wang had begun snoring.

"So it's true that heavy people are easy sleepers!" I said, but Xianmeng did not reply and, soon, he too was snoring. How could I fall asleep under these circumstances? A faint moon shone through a cloudy sky, its dull glow barely spilling into the room. Now and then, a gentle wind rattled the latticework in front of the window. Inside our room, the sound of snoring reverberated, now high, now low, drawn out one moment and hurried the next. Then, all of a sudden, it was as if someone were tapping against the glass on the outer side of the corridor, three times total. I listened carefully, but the sound was already gone. But just when I rolled over in a desperate effort to find a good sleeping position, there it was again: three knocks. There really seemed to be someone out there, knocking against the glass panes. I was thinking of waking up Mr. Wang and Xianmeng, but then felt it would be better not to make a fuss about nothing. Instead, I listened again carefully. The sound was gone. But after a little while, there it was again, this time seven or eight rapid knocks. It was really bizarre.

I groped for the flashlight next to my pillow and shone its beam on the shōji panel. Again the sound was gone, this time for quite a while, at least the time it takes to smoke a couple of cigarettes. Then there were five more knocks on the windowpanes in the corridor. This time, it sounded almost rhythmical: knock, knock, knock, knock—knock, and then after a short while, it went: knock, knock—knock, knock—knock. Again I thought of waking Mr. Wang and Xianmeng, but then I suddenly heard the faint sound of someone sighing. By now, my curiosity had triumphed over my fear, and I decided against waking up the two. I held my breath and listened attentively. There it was again: knock, knock—knock, knock—knock, knock, knock. How strange! Hesitant about what to do, I once more shone the flashlight onto the shōji panels by the door of our room.

All of a sudden, I heard someone whimpering. Then the whimpering turned into a low weeping. I now could hear that it was from a woman. All this was becoming more and more bizarre, I thought. Was I reliving a ghost story from *Strange Tales from a Chinese Studio*? Or was it possible that I was dreaming? I shone the flashlight on my hand and squeezed my fingers. It all felt pretty real. Just then, the knocking on the window could be heard again: knock, knock, knock, knock, knock, knock, and the sound of weeping became even more pronounced. Was I just imagining it? Or, it suddenly occurred to me, could it possibly be Xiancheng whom I heard crying? I carefully listened again, but the sound had stopped. I waited silently, and after a while, I heard a faint sigh, followed by suppressed sobbing. This time, I heard it clearly. There was no doubt that it was Xiancheng who was sobbing, but why was she crying? I wanted to call out to her, but then thought that she might feel embarrassed. I was also afraid that I would wake the others. Could it be that she had wanted to sleep upstairs and was unhappy that she now had to sleep downstairs? Or was it because there had been an unpleasantry between her and Cunmei before they went to bed?

I was so preoccupied by thinking about Xiancheng that I no

longer paid attention to the knocking or the snoring of my room-mates, but then I heard again four fast-paced knocks. Shortly after, I heard the sound of a door being slid open in the adjacent room. I saw the beam of a flashlight in the corridor and thought that it must be Xiancheng who was going outside. I sat up, and listened attentively. Maybe the person knocking on the glass was Xiancheng's lover? But this late and this high up in the mountains? That would be grotesque. Could it be Dawen? Ridiculous. Why should he come knocking on the window this late? But maybe they knew each other before, and they were playing some kind of trick on us? A ghost? Could a ghost be knocking on the window? Maybe Xiancheng was also a ghost?

The more I thought about it the more perplexing it all seemed. Suddenly there were three more knocks, this time very faint ones. That brought me back to my senses. Maybe Xiancheng had merely gone to the bathroom, and it was me who was see-ing ghosts! But I had clearly heard her weeping. Sitting on the tatami mat, I had a cigarette. I thought that if by the time I had finished my smoke she had not come back, I would go out and have a look. But then, having not even finished half of my cigarette, I began to put on my pants, my socks, my coat, and the padded kimono. I then tucked the flashlight into the inside of the kimono, quietly slid open the door, and went out. I slid shut the door behind me and walked back through the corridor. When I got to its end, I put on my shoes and hurried to the front door. The front door was unlocked and I went out, pulling it shut behind.

I went back to the fork in the road and stood there for a moment. I turned on my flashlight and saw Xiancheng on the road leading down. When she noticed that someone was shining a light at her, she also turned on hers and shone it up toward me. It was like two ships in the night signaling at each other. She remained where she was and I walked over to her. She was very composed and did not seem upset that I had followed her.

"So you heard it too?" she asked.

"Of course," I said. "What on earth was that?"

"Strange," she said, gazing at the forest on the mountain slope opposite us. "Very strange!"

Then she fell silent. I shone my flashlight at our hotel. I noticed that the glass panes of the corridor leading to our rooms could be seen from the road. A deep creek ran in the middle. I walked back until I stood in front of the corridor and shone my flashlight on the glass panes. And then I realized: A branch from a tree growing on the bank of the creek was tapping against the window whenever it was swayed by the wind. I wanted to share my realization with Xiancheng, who had already walked downhill a little. She was standing in front of a big rock and was looking into the distance.

I caught up with her and said, "Xiancheng, it turns out a tree branch that was swayed by the wind was tapping against the window."

"Listen, listen!" Not only was she not paying attention to what I was saying, she seemed to reproach me for talking.

I listened for a moment and said, "The wind."

"Listen, listen!"

"The trees," I said. "When the wind runs through them, they naturally …"

"Listen!"

All I heard was the sound of the wind whispering through the trees, but I remained silent.

"Aren't you hearing the wailing sound from the all-souls trees? 'Oh love, oh sorrow' is what they are calling."

Once she had said this, it really seemed as if I could discern a faint 'oh love, oh sorrow' amidst the sound of the wind. I nodded. She suddenly sat down on the big rock in front of us and started to cry.

"Xiancheng, what's the matter?" I asked her, but she just went on crying.

"What's the matter, Xiancheng?" I could not think of anything to console her and said, "Let's go back."

She took out a handkerchief and wiped her tears but continued to cry.

"What's going on, Xiancheng? If you trust me, then please tell me! I will do all I can to help you," I said to her. She seemed to be listening to me and calmed down a little.

"If there is anything Xianmeng can do for you, but you can't talk to him yourself, I will talk to him on your behalf. You know that he and I have been friends for more than a decade. We can talk about anything."

She was quite composed now and so I continued, "There is no one here but you and me. If you want to share a secret with me, I'll promise that I won't tell anyone. We all carry some old wounds. Sometimes telling a friend about them can bring some comfort, even if it won't help the healing. Instead of crying all by yourself, why don't you tell me what's on your mind?"

She remained silent until she suddenly raised her head, her tear-filled eyes wide open, and fearfully said, "Listen, listen!"

We listened for a while. Finally, she said in a stifled, low voice, "You hear the all-souls tree? It's the wailing of my boyfriend."

"Your boyfriend?" I asked. "Where is he?"

"In Jiujiang, in Jiangxi province," she replied. "It's too long a story to tell."

"Don't worry!" I said as I sat down by her side. "Just keep going, maybe I can help you. I can even go to Jiujiang for you, if you need me to. I have nothing better to do anyway."

She wiped her eyes with her handkerchief and gave me a glance before lowering her eyes. Then, clutching her damp handkerchief, she began to tell me in a low and husky voice what had happened to her and her boyfriend.

"We were both attending the same middle school. He was three grades my senior. His father and my father knew each other and when the two of us became friends, neither family had any objections."

"The two of you must have been very happy," I said, but she paid no attention and, after taking a deep breath, continued.

"We became a couple when he was in his last semester of high school. I myself had only six months of junior middle school left until I could graduate. At that time, I contracted a mild case of pneumonia, but it wasn't very serious. I was afraid that if he knew, he wouldn't love me anymore, and so I did not tell him. He was planning to go to *Beiping after graduation to sit for the university entrance exams. I had a maternal uncle and aunt in Beiping who liked me a lot. They often told me to come live with them in Beiping and to attend school there. Because of them, I knew that if I were to go study there, my parents would not object.

"And so, the two of us made plans to go to Beiping together in the summer following our graduation. But because of my poor health, I often had to take leaves of absence. My schoolwork suffered, and so I was afraid that I would not be able to graduate. Not being able to graduate would of course mean an enormous loss of face, but what I feared most was that he would despise me and that my parents would no longer let me go to Beiping to continue my studies. That's why I became extremely diligent. Who could have known that once our graduation exams were done, I immediately began to cough blood and run a fever? The doctor said that the disease had flared up and that I would have to be hospitalized for at least six months and so I was admitted to a sanatorium.

"I was devastated, for my dream of going to Beiping with him was shattered. When I received my graduation certificate, I was crying in my bed and none of my family members could do anything about it. When he came to see me later, he said that he had decided to wait for six months or a year and that once my disease was cured we would go to Beiping together. I told him he could not do that. There were no decent universities in Jiujiang, how could he forsake his plan of going to university on my behalf? He said that there was no problem if he postponed by a year, and that he had already made arrangements with a primary school where he could teach. His family naturally objected to his plan. My father was also not in favor of it and thought that he ought to go to Beiping first and start university. I could follow him the year after, once my disease was cured. We were both still young and there was no reason why we should fear being separated. Only my mother was grateful to him, because she knew that he did this out of love for me and to comfort me. My mother knew that had he gone, I certainly would have been extremely sad, which could not have been good for my state of health. And so he postponed the university entrance exam and instead taught at a primary school. Once his classes were over, he'd run right over to the hospital. He would often do his grading there. He was very healthy and was good at sports. He had never been sick and was not afraid of catching my disease."

At this point in her story, Xiancheng again began to cry. "At that time," she sobbed, "I was so muddleheaded. How could I let him kiss me all the time?" She rested a little, and then continued.

"After six months, I had some X-rays taken, and to everyone's surprise, the wound had healed. But then suddenly he took sick. I had infected him, and his condition turned very serious. He ran a high fever and every day coughed blood. After not even two months, he was so thin he was hardly himself anymore. And then, all of a sudden, there were some changes with my father's work and he wanted the whole family to move to Beiping. What could I have done? We weren't married yet, and there was no way I would be allowed to stay behind on my own in Jiujiang to look after my boyfriend. Again and again I pleaded with my mother, but she said there was nothing to be done. People are always selfish, even a mother as good as mine. She said exactly the same as what his parents had said, that I could just as well wait for him in Beiping while starting high school, and that once he had recovered he would follow us to Beiping for university. I felt terrible. After all, he had delayed his university entrance exams on my behalf, had contracted my illness, and then in the end I ..." She started to cry again and gazed at the dark sky. After a while, she continued.

"But he is so wonderful, and not at all selfish. He told me not to be sad and urged me to go to Beiping. He said that he would be fine as long as I wrote him two letters a week."

At this point, Xiancheng paused again and wiped her eyes. She looked at me and said, "But in reality he was so weak that he could not even write letters by himself. But there was nothing I could do, and once everything had been decided, I asked the nurses in the hospital for help. They were very nice and promised to write letters to me on his behalf and not to let him write them by himself. When I went to see him to say goodbye on the day before my departure, the sky was overcast and rainy. I couldn't stop crying. He kept smiling and comforted me, but ..."

Xiancheng abruptly stopped. She turned her upper body and gazed at the mountain ridges, listening attentively. Then she said hurriedly, "Listen, listen!"

She fell silent again, and after a while continued under sobs: "When I stepped out of his hospital room and the nurse was closing the door, I heard him utter the words 'oh love, oh sorrow!' I wanted to go back in and see, but my mother was waiting for me and pulled me away once I had stepped out of the room. This parting of ours was five years ago."

"And he has been in the hospital in Jiujiang all this time?" I asked. Xiancheng nodded her head.

"Do you often receive letters from him?"

"Yes, but they are written by the nurses. He sometimes adds a word or two in his own hand," Xiancheng replied. "After the war of resistance against Japan was over and I had graduated from high school, I did not want to go on to university. I wanted to wait for him and attend with him, and so I went to work as an assistant in a bank. After one year, I was promoted to regular clerk, but then my father died, and all our savings were eaten up by inflation. Originally, I had wanted to quit my job and go back to Jiujiang to be with him, but by then my work was feeding our family and I could not quit. And then, not long after, I was dispatched to Taiwan...."

"Oh love, oh sorrow!"

I suddenly also could hear that sound in the mountains. It was deep and mournful, full of grief and anxiety, sorrow and despair. It sent a shiver down my spine. For a long time I did not utter a word. Neither did she.

"I am sure he will be fine," I finally said.

"I also used to think so," she said, "but tonight, having heard this sound, I am scared. I feel it might be a bad omen."

"I think you are too superstitious," I consoled her. "Your mind is playing tricks on you. What I really heard sounded more like 'All right, tomorrow,'" I lied.

"'All right, tomorrow'?" She suddenly stared at me, eyes wide open. "What do you mean?"

"I am sure his illness will get better and he will soon be all right," I said uneasily.

"You're right. I let him down, I am unworthy of his love." She started to cry again.

Suddenly I realized that when I had said that his illness would be getting better, I had caused this sensitive lady to think of the ill-fated heroine Lin Daiyu in *Dream of the Red Chamber*! I was extremely uneasy and did not dare say anything else. After a long while, I finally urged her to get up. "Let's go back and get some sleep. The others might wake up and think the two of us ..." Afraid that I would again say the wrong thing, I left it at that. But she had understood and probably thought that my misgivings were justified. She let me help her get up, and, turning on my flashlight, I led her back to the hotel.

We closed the front door behind us and took off our shoes at the entrance to the corridor. Just then I was suddenly overcome by dread that someone might have noticed us. I did not know whether she felt the same, but at least she no longer seemed to be paying attention to the moaning sounds from outside and very cautiously tiptoed back into her room. When I returned to my room, I was overcome by an indescribable fatigue. And even though Mr. Wang's snoring was even louder, and Xianmeng's heavy breathing had not abated in the least, I immediately fell asleep.

When I awoke the next morning, everybody had already gotten up. Mr. Wang said I really slept like a log. He said he had woken up at four in the morning and originally had wanted to wake us all up to see the sunrise, but when he had stepped outside and seen that the sky was covered with thick clouds, he had decided not to wake us. He said he had gone back to bed, but somehow could no longer fall asleep.

Breakfast was taken in the same upstairs room with the enclosed balcony. Xiancheng was the last to come up.

"You look rested," I said to her.

"Thank you," she replied with a composed smile, but I knew that her mind was far from composed. After breakfast, Mr. Wang's friend took the lead and we went sightseeing. We saw a lot of scenic spots and historic sites, temples, and an old lumberyard. The weather was fair. The sky would be overcast one moment and clear the next, leaden one moment and then bright again a moment later. At every step we took photos. Only Xiancheng did not want to be in any of them. Every now and then, Ms. Nie and Ms. Li would grab her arm to have her be in a photo, but each time she tactfully declined. This was something I never quite understood. Xianmeng and Cuimei naturally were used to her behavior and at times made excuses for her.

We were a lively bunch out there on the mountain. Mr. Wang and Ms. Li had a great sense of humor, while Ms. Nie was a bit of a hypochondriac and from time to time would throw pills into her mouth. Yesterday, everyone had been tired from the journey up the mountain, but now, we were all well rested and everyone was joking around. Xianmeng was a man with a broad range of interests and could provide the backstory to each historic site we visited. Cunmei was always in high spirits when she was with him, and Mr. Shi kept telling us little anecdotes, all the while pointing out things that deserved attention. He told us the height of a certain tree or the age of a certain temple. Only Xiancheng remained silent all along. She did not join our laughter and showed no interest in anything. She just tagged along, head lowered. Dawen time and again would walk next to her. It seemed that he was trying to find an opportunity to talk to her, but none presented itself. Eventually, when she abruptly took off her raincoat, Dawen stretched out his arm to take it from her. She graciously thanked him, but thereafter did not utter another word.

I was still holding on to the branch from the all-souls tree that she had given me the previous day and that was all the more precious to me now. There were many such trees along the way, and I broke off a branch for her, saying, "Here, let me give you one as well."

She accepted it with a smile and held on to it in silence. We wandered around for about two hours and then went back to the station to take the same diesel engine down the mountain. The journey continued to be lively and interesting. Only Xiancheng sat in a corner and gazed at the distant mountains and forests. I suddenly wondered whether maybe she was still hearing the sound of wailing. I listened carefully. No, there was nothing. There was only the sound of our diesel engine swiftly traveling along its rails. The train was going down at a speed three times faster than going up the previous day, sweeping past countless mountain ridges, charging through light clouds and thick fog, and passing through tunnel after tunnel.

We arrived in Chiayi at two in the afternoon. The women went to the hotel to rest, Dawen went to Taichung to consult with the university, and Mr. Wang and Mr. Shi attended to their business at the factory. That left Xianmeng and me to wander around Chiayi for a while. I very much wanted to talk to him about the matter concerning Xiancheng, but the city streets were not the right place to talk and so I did not broach the topic. And Xiancheng? She neither took a nap nor explored Chiayi with us. Cunmei later told me that she was alone in her room, writing a letter.

The rest of the trip proceeded as planned. Mr. Wang had bought us sleeper tickets for the ten o'clock night train, which meant that we could have dinner prior to boarding. I urged everyone to have a little drink so that we would sleep better on the train. I knew that Mr. Wang liked to drink. Xianmeng, on the other hand, drank little, and I drank even less. The women all only had three tiny cups, but to my surprise, Xiancheng turned out to be a match for Mr. Wang. She had not said a word all day, but now she was merrily drinking away with him. Had Dawen not gone to Taichung, he certainly would have happily joined them.

In the end, Xiancheng was more than a little drunk, but she still wanted to keep drinking. Mr. Wang himself would have liked to keep going, but he had enough experience to know that Xiancheng had had enough and tried to stop her. Xianmeng and I joined in the effort and urged her to stop. Mr. Wang then divided what was left in the wine pitcher between everyone and we all drank up. Xiancheng was drunk. She seemed to be thinking that it was Xianmeng who had not wanted her to drink anymore and was quite upset. She sat there in silence until suddenly a shiny tear appeared in the corner of her eye. Cunmei and I helped her to the sofa to take a nap, and we hastily finished our dinner. Then we got on the train. The wine had done its trick. I for one slept really well that night. I only woke up twice, each time when the train had come to a stop in a station. Both times, I peered over at Xiancheng, who also seemed to be sound asleep. We arrived in Taipei early the next morning and said our fare-wells once we had stepped out of the railway station.

I took a morning shower and went back to sleep for a while. When I woke up, I couldn't stop thinking of Xiancheng. I wanted to go and talk to Xianmeng and Cunmei. I was not going to tell them everything that had occurred two nights ago, but we had to think of a way to help Xiancheng and her boyfriend. However, after lunch, a friend came over and asked me to accompany him to visit a friend of mine who was teaching at National Taiwan University. My friend was hoping that I could introduce him, because he wanted to go to the university library and look at some books on birds. Birds were that friend's only interest, and wherever he went he wanted to learn more about the local species. I pitied him almost as much as I pitied Xiancheng, and so I accompanied him. In that way, the day came to an end.

The next day happened to be a Sunday. I figured that Xiancheng would not have to go to work that day, so I decided to go to Xianmeng's place early in the morning. If Xiancheng happened to be at the house of Xianmeng's brother, I would first talk with Xianmeng, and then we could go to his brother's together. The front door was wide open. I walked in and went straight to the living room. To my surprise, the living room was full of people, some of whom I had met before and some whom I did not know. Xianmeng's brother and his wife were there, and Cunmei was sitting together with some older ladies. Everyone was crying and the atmosphere was extremely solemn. No one said a word. I felt at a loss and, because I could spot neither Xianmeng nor Xiancheng among those seated, left the living room. In the corridor I ran into Xianmeng.

"What's all this about?" I asked in a low voice.

"Yesterday just when we got home she received a telegram." Xianmeng must have assumed that I already knew what had happened, having just walked out of the living room.

"What telegram?"

"The one they had sent to Xiancheng."

"What happened?"

"Her boyfriend has passed away."

"Passed away? So he did die after all.... How about Xiancheng? Is she at home?" I asked.

"She killed herself."

"Killed herself?"

"Who would have thought," Xianmeng said. "After I had helped her decipher the telegram, she did not cry. She just sat on the sofa, her face twitching. I wanted to talk to her and console her, but she paid no attention to me. After a while, she went to her room, but she came out again about half an hour later. She was holding her knitting gear and began to knit. By then, I had already told Cunmei about the telegram, and Cunmei naturally also tried to console her, but Xiancheng remained silent and only knitted away. When it was almost time to eat, she suddenly got up at said, 'Ah, it's done at last.'"

"After lunch," Xianmeng continued, "she said she was going to the bank. We knew she had an odd temper and did not dare to bother her. She came back at seven, had dinner, and then stayed upstairs by herself. We asked the maid to check on her, and she told us Xiancheng was writing a letter. At half past nine, she came down to the kitchen to burn a pile of letters. The maid said Xiancheng had been very cheerful and had chatted with her while burning them. Afterward, she asked the maid for hot water so that she could take a bath. When she was done, we all went to bed. This morning, the maid went into her room and noticed that there was something not quite right about the color of her face. She called me in and I immediately telephoned for a doctor. The doctor said she had been dead for at least three hours."

"What did she swallow to kill herself?" I asked.

"We did not find anything in her room, but in the bathroom we later found three empty bottles of sleeping pills. She must have swallowed the contents all at once."

"Did she leave a note?"

"Just a very simple one," Xianmeng replied. "Aside from thanking us, she asked us to send what little jewelry and US dollars she owned to her younger brothers."

"She's got brothers?"

"Two," Xianmeng told me. "Both of them are in Beiping."

"Working?"

"Both are studying."

Just then, several young people whom I did not know arrived. They exchanged greetings with Xianmeng and I learned that they were Xiancheng's colleagues who had come to find out more about what had happened. Xianmeng asked everyone to sit in the veranda and I sat down with them. I learned that Xiancheng indeed had gone to the bank in the afternoon of the previous day. One of the women said that Xiancheng had boxed a woolen sweater she had knitted and asked one of her colleagues to go to the post office and mail it. She waited for the colleague to return and stayed until the end of the workday. The bank holiday had only lasted until the day before yesterday, but Xiancheng had also taken off yesterday morning. Apparently, she had gaily chatted with her colleagues about the scenery at Mount Ali. No one could have guessed what was on her mind. From their conversation, I also learned that those sleeping pills came from the stock of a pharmacist who was a friend of theirs and who had asked Xiancheng and some of the others to help him sell them. For that reason, a few boxes were kept in the bank. Apparently, they were all kept in a hard-to-reach place together with some boxes of vitamins. Could it be, they wondered, that she had mistakenly …?

Xianmeng told us that Xiancheng had already been cremated.

"Cremated?" I asked.

"Yes," Xianmeng replied. "There is a place here that provides cremation in accordance with Buddhist burial ritual."

Addressing again Xiancheng's colleagues, he said, "Tomorrow, there will be a simple Buddhist ceremony at Hulong Temple on Hulong Street."

The next day, I went to Hulong Temple. Xianmeng took me to a hall in the back where the ashes were kept. There was a line of long tables on top of which were placed candleholders, incense burners, flower vases for paper flowers, and a row of small cups filled with tea. There were wooden shelves on all four sides that were divided into lots of small squares, and on each shelf was a small, yellow porcelain urn. Each urn had a little red paper slip pasted on top. Xianmeng led me in front of one of the urns and pointed at it. I read the words "deceased cousin Xiancheng …," but my eyes were already blurry. I no longer saw a yellow vase, but instead a face with a slightly protruding forehead, pointed lower jaw, upright nose, big eyes, and delicate eyebrows. My gaze remained fixed for a long time. Then I placed the branch of the all-souls tree she had given me into one of the vases with paper flowers. The branch was already wilted, but there still remained some leaves on it. On their back, I had written the following words:

Oh love, oh sorrow! It is in moments of great sorrow that we grasp the meaning of deep love. Yet it is also when love is at its deepest that we experience true sorrow.

來高升路的一個女人
When Ah Heung Came to Gousing Road

By 1965, the year this story was first published, Hong Kong's population had risen from roughly half a million by the end of World War II in 1945 to almost four million. At first, most of the new arrivals had been refugees fleeing the fighting in China that had flared up again between the Nationalists and the Communists after Japan's surrender. In the wake of the founding of the People's Republic of China in 1949, many more left China for political reasons, like Xu Xu himself. In subsequent years, despite the eventual tightening of immigration control on both sides of the border, there was a constant trickle of economic migrants to Hong Kong, especially during years of particular hardship in China, like the years of famine that followed the Great Leap Forward (1958–62). Hong Kong's colonial government tended to repatriate immigrants caught in the border area, yet it tolerated immigrants who managed to reach the urban areas of Hong Kong, a policy that remained in effect until 1980. These immigrants, like Ah Heung and her two friends in the story, fueled much of Hong Kong's economic growth in the postwar period.

Like Ah Heung, most of the immigrants tended to come from the bordering province of Guangdong. Its capital *Canton, also known as Guangzhou, is where Ah Heung's two friends in the story are from. By the early 1960s, Hong Kong's economy was growing rapidly, in part because of the development of light industry, particularly electronics. The fact that one of the two friends dreams of owning an electrical supplies shop appears to reflect this development. Betting on dogs and horses was a popular pastime in Hong Kong, as was frequenting local operas sung in Cantonese or watching movies from Hong Kong or Hollywood. Hong Kong in the story is depicted as a city where an individual's hard work and dexterity might lead to a better life—the word "Gousing," which literally means "rising high," is not only a likely name for a road on mountainous Hong Kong Island but also a pun on Ah Heung's ultimate fate. However, Ah Heung also displays a moral integrity toward her friends that readers would have associated with a traditional *jianghu* 江湖 spirit, a kind of chivalry associated with legendary bands of itinerants roaming the rivers (*jiang*) and lakes (*hu*) of southern China.

Gousing Road is a steep little alley on Hong Kong Island. It cascades up a slope and near the top assumes the shape of a W. At the top of the slope, all the houses belong to rich folks. Because Gousing Road is lined on both sides with high rises, it is not directly exposed to the sun, and as a result it is a little cooler there on hot days.

At the entrance to Gousing Road there used to be three street stalls. One of them was a stall selling leather shoes. The shoemaker, Old Gam, was a friendly and hardworking chap in his fifties. He usually had more work than he could finish in one day. Even though he was sewing shoes day in, day out with his head bent down low, he knew a fair bit of gossip about most of the families in the neighborhood. He was a cheerful sort and liked to chat while working. Next to Old Gam's stall was a hardware stall that specialized in cutting keys. Business at times was good, and at other times it was slow. Its owner, Mah Daksing, was a clever but lazy fellow who was still in his twenties. Sometimes people called him to help them open their doors. The last one was a small stall selling potted flowers and miniature trees. Its owner, Sing Zyunfuk, was the youngest of the three and, like Daksing, was originally from *Canton. The two had been primary school classmates, and he had been able to come here to set up his stall largely thanks to Daksing's connections. When Daksing had to go and help someone with a lock, Zyunfuk would look after his stall for him, and when Daksing did not have anything to do, the two of them would play chess.

When Ah Heung first showed up in Gousing Road, Daksing and Zyunfuk were immediately taken in by her beautiful face and her long braids. Old Gam told them that she was the servant girl of the Si family from across the street. From then on, Old Gam noticed that Daksing paid close attention to Ah Heung. Old Gam sometimes would even joke with him about it, yet none of them ever had an opportunity to talk to her.

But then one day, Ah Heung came to Daksing's stall to have a key cut. Daksing and Zyunfuk were playing chess at the time, and Daksing asked her to come back after a few hours to pick up the key, but Ah Heung said she wanted to wait.

"I have lost my key to the main gate. This one is the key of the lady of the house." She had borrowed the key to make a copy, but she did not want her mistress to know. That's why she wanted to take it right back. Daksing reluctantly had to interrupt his game of chess. He got up and, working his file, began to duplicate the key. Ah Heung waited by the side and started to chat with Zyunfuk.

"Isn't your mistress the young lady who drives a car by herself?" Zyunfuk asked.

"Yes, that's her," Ah Heung replied. "She is good-looking, isn't she?"

"Mr. Si is quite a bit older than her," Old Gam threw in.

"Mr. Si is in his fifties and she is his second wife. She used to be a dancing girl in Taiwan."

"That's what I guessed," Old Gam said. "When they moved here last year, I already could tell."

"Don't they have kids?" Zyunfuk asked.

"He has two kids with his first wife, but when Mr. Si married our mistress, his first wife was furious. She took the children and went to live in America."

"Do they have a lot of money?" Zyunfuk kept asking.

"Of course! How else could two people afford to live in such a big house?" Old Gam said.

"Zyunfuk, when you strike it rich someday, you should take a cue from Mr. Si," Daksing said as he was treading on the wheel that powered his file.

"Seeing them live like that, they must be worth at least a few hundred thousand," Zyunfuk said. "That's not bad."

"A few hundred thousand? Gotta be more than that!" Ah Heung exclaimed. "Our mistress's jewelry alone is worth more than that. That diamond ring on her hand is worth at least eighteen grand."

Daksing was done with the duplicate. Ah Heung took the two keys, paid, and quickly left.

From then on, whenever he saw Ah Heung leave the house, Zyunfuk would deliberately step into the street and wait for her. Pretending that he had run into her by chance, he would walk with her a little. Once, when she went to Central, he accompanied her and on their way back, the two had some tea and snacks. Gradually, he and Ah Heung got to know each other better.

II

Zyunfuk had come to Hong Kong from Canton two years earlier. He had a distant relative in Hong Kong, a cousin of his father's. This relative owned a small nursery in Shau Kei Wan where he grew flowers and cultivated miniature trees that he then sold. Zyunfuk lived with his father's cousin, but he did not know a thing about cultivating flowers. Moreover, he was not interested. In Canton, he had been an apprentice to an electrician and had worked at an appliances store for a while after he came to Hong Kong. But he had not gotten along with his boss and had soon left. He had long wanted to run a small shop for electrical supplies on his own, selling light bulbs and fixing faulty wiring, but he had always lacked the initial capital and so the opportunity had never presented itself.

Because he was friends with Daksing and often met up with him, he eventually got some potted flowers and miniature trees from his uncle and set up a small stall on Gousing Road. He had a good profit margin, and even though business was not exactly great, he still could make enough money to get by. Other than playing chess together, Zyunfuk and Daksing also cooperated in placing high-stakes bets on dogs and horses at betting shops. Seeing that they often won, even Old Gam would sometimes chip in and try his luck. They lived simple lives, and even though they did not have much, they were at ease with themselves and quite happy. But all that began to change after Ah Heung showed up on Gousing Road.

From that day on, it seemed that all their conversation invariably focused on Ah Heung. After Zyunfuk had become acquainted with her, he told Daksing and Old Gam everything that happened between them. Daksing and Old Gam would then offer their opinion. The way Old Gam saw it, Ah Heung had at least four or five thousand Hong Kong dollars in savings. If Zyunfuk could marry her, then they would easily be able to open an electrical supplies stall. That was what Zyunfuk had often talked about and what he really wanted to do. Selling things like light bulbs and sockets, small table lamps and lampshades, and fixing lights or installing appliances in the neighborhood certainly would be good business. Old Gam began to closely observe Ah Heung's comings and goings. When he saw her leave or enter Gousing Road, he would tell Zyunfuk. Zyunfuk often asked Daksing to look after his stall so that he could accompany Ah Heung shopping and carry her groceries for her. Ah Heung also frequently came over to chat with them. At times, she also asked them for help with some small matters.

The days passed, and even though Zyunfuk often went to the movies with Ah Heung or had a late-night snack with her, he just never found the right moment to tell her how he felt about her. What was more, Ah Heung was very generous, and when they grabbed a bite in the evening, she usually snatched up the bill. Ah Heung was a straightforward and cheerful girl. She rarely talked about herself but liked to talk about her mistress. She liked her mistress a lot, and her mistress seemed to like her a lot. Her mistress was from Shanghai, but in 1949 she and her family had left for Taiwan. She later became a dancing girl and met up with a lot of wealthy and powerful men. All this she shared with Ah Heung, who listened with great interest. Ah Heung then told these stories to Zyunfuk, who in turn told them to Daksing and Old Gam.

Old Gam was a man with good judgment and he soon realized that Zyunfuk was not an ideal match for Ah Heung. Zyunfuk himself, however, did not. He was convinced that he had fallen head over heels in love. Every day, he yearned to see Ah Heung. He would ask her out to see a local opera or have a snack in the evening, but when he was together with Ah Heung, he did not really have anything to say to her. Ah Heung, on the other hand, in a natural and unaffected manner, chatted about her mistress or her master. She was happy to be friends with Zyunfuk, but it seemed she was oblivious to his feelings toward her.

When Zyunfuk recounted all that had happened the previous evenings to Daksing and Old Gam, Old Gam remarked, "The way I see it, Ah Heung is a very smart girl. I am sure she's been influenced by that mistress of hers from Shanghai. She's probably quite cocky, and I guess she won't get married for the time being. And when she does get married, she'll want to marry someone rich."

Hearing Old Gam talk like this, Daksing felt pity for Zyunfuk and said, "But you have to at least tell her how you feel. I mean, if she didn't like you, she wouldn't go out with you. Have you maybe ... held her hand or put your arm around her waist or kissed her on the cheek?"

"I have often held her hand, and she is fine with that, but when I try to put my arm around her waist, she pushes me away," Zyunfuk replied. "Once when I asked her to go for a walk, she told me that what she hated most was seeing all those secretive couples hiding out in the narrow alleyways. I never tried that again afterward."

"I think you might as well put your cards on the table," Daksing said. "Why don't you propose to her and see what she says?"

"Right, tomorrow I am going to.... I'll see what she says...."

If she turns me down, I'll just forget the whole thing and won't ask her out anymore."

It seemed that he had made up his mind.

III

And thus, seated in a small booth inside a café, Zyunfuk opened his heart to Ah Heung. He began by telling her that he loved her, and then went on to tell her how he imagined their life together. He told her that he was an aspiring electrician, and that he wanted to open an electrical supplies store and establish a family. Finally, he said he hoped that he and Ah Heung would spend the rest of their lives together.

After he had said everything he had wanted to say, he expected Ah Heung to be moved by his words. Ah Heung, however, patted his hand in the way an adult does to a child and began to laugh out loud.

"What's the matter?" Zyunfuk asked.

"You want to get married? Well, then you should find yourself a rich girl. You are poor, I am poor, what's the use of us getting married? Hasn't any of that crossed your mind? You might be older than me, but clearly not any wiser."

"You want to get married to someone rich?"

"I don't want to get married at all yet," Ah Heung said laughing. "But when I do get married, I naturally want to marry someone with money. I was born into a poor family. I have never once worn a pretty dress or lived in a nice house. For a woman, getting married is like being born a second time. Would I want to be born into a pauper's house again? You really are something! Look at my mistress, Ms. Si. She married a man with wealth, and she is now living the good life."

"That Ms. Si of yours is the concubine of an old geezer; what's so great about that?"

"She can do or have whatever she wants. If she wants to

sleep she can sleep, if she wants to have fun she can have fun. I think she is the happiest person in the world!"

"But I love you!" Zyunfuk exclaimed.

"I like you too, and it's because I like you that I don't want you to be led astray. Quite frankly, you won't be able to support me. As for me, I am still young. I have so many dreams and so many things that I want, but for any of that I first of all need money."

"Ah Heung, I really didn't expect …," but Zyunfuk was cut short by Ah Heung.

"I don't care if you think I am shallow or that I don't understand love. What I do know is this: We are poor folks, and poor folks can't afford to fall in love. Poor folks shouldn't talk morals either. Us poor folks first need to have money, because only then do we stop being beggars."

"Are you done, Ah Heung?" Zyunfuk had never heard anything like this before. He suddenly looked at Ah Heung with different eyes. "Ah Heung, you might be younger," he said in surprise, "but you sure are much savvier than me."

"Now that you know, we can still be friends," Ah Heung said. "To tell you the truth, I have learned all this from my mistress. She's very good to me, and she explained all these things to me. I was engaged to a cousin of mine. He left his home in Guangdong province and came to Hong Kong to get married with me. I discussed the whole matter with my mistress. She told me to give him some money and break off the engagement. I followed her advice and that's why I am free now. My fiancé later married a different girl who gave birth to two children. They live in Hung Hom and they both work their asses off. Wouldn't you say that I was lucky that I didn't fall into that trap?"

"Maybe you should become a dancing girl then," Zyunfuk said with a sneer. "That way you can get to know a bunch of rich guys."

"I actually thought about that, but my mistress said that

once a woman is a dancing girl, she will always be treated like one. She said she'll introduce me to someone wealthy when the time comes," Ah Heung proudly said, laughing.

Zyunfuk felt that there wasn't anything left for him to say. He felt rather crestfallen. But then Ah Heung said, "Don't be sad because of this. If you want, we can still be good friends. We are all poor and we should all help each other. You are also still young; why do you want to get married now? If you really want to inflict suffering on others and yourself, wait until you have at least eighty or a hundred thousand Hong Kong dollars. By then, it will still be early enough to find yourself a wife."

Ah Heung took a sip of tea and said, "But now I really have to get back home."

IV

The next day, when Zyunfuk told Daksing and Old Gam about his hapless marriage proposal, they were equally surprised about Ah Heung. None of the three had thought that their little girl had such grand ambitions. Daksing concluded that Ah Heung's behavior betrayed her upbringing in mainland China, which is why she knew all that talk about poor people having to free themselves. Old Gam, on the other hand, felt that she had been molded by her mistress, which is why she knew all about how to get rich.

From then on, Daksing's and Old Gam's attitude toward Ah Heung was no longer the same. Not only did they no longer encourage Zyunfuk to pursue her, they also no longer teased him about her. They talked about her as if she was part of the family and never again used frivolous language. When Ah Heung happened to come by to say hello, they also acted differently from before. They talked more, but also feared her a little. Zyunfuk, however, no longer asked her out and was even afraid of running into her. When he saw her coming over, he would find an excuse and clear off. Ah Heung, on the contrary, visited them more frequently, and whenever she did, she chatted and laughed with Daksing and Old Gam.

About two weeks later, Old Gam suddenly got sick and did not show up for work. Old Gam lived alone with his wife, who came by to let Daksing know. Daksing went to see Old Gam right away. Old Gam had already taken some herbal medicine and said that he only had a slight fever. He would be back at work again tomorrow, he said.

But the next day, Old Gam still did not show up for work. Just when Daksing was thinking that he'd go to see him again in the afternoon, Ah Heung happened to come by. When she heard that Old Gam was sick, she said that her mistress often went to see a doctor by the name of Joeng who was really good. She quickly ran home and came back with the address. She handed it to Daksing and insisted that he had to take Old Gam there in the afternoon. She then took out a hundred-dollar bill from her leather purse and gave it to Daksing. It was meant to cover Old Gam's medical expenses.

Daksing was moved. When he went to see Old Gam in the afternoon, he told him that Ah Heung had insisted he take him to see Dr. Joeng and that she had given him a hundred dollars. Old Gam absolutely did not want to go.

He said he'd be fine if he rested for a couple of days. Daksing, however, didn't want Old Gam to be ungrateful to Ah Heung. There'd be plenty of opportunities to return the favor, and he could worry about that after he had gotten better. And so, Daksing accompanied Old Gam to see the doctor, who gave him an injection and prescribed him some medicine. The visit and the medicine cost them thirty dollars, and Dr. Joeng asked Old Gam to come back again after two days. When they left the doctor's office, Old Gam wanted Daksing to return the remaining seventy dollars to Ah Heung. He said he'd be fine on his own and that he did not need to see the doctor again.

The next day, Ah Heung stopped by to see Daksing and asked about Old Gam's condition. Daksing told her what the doctor had said and that Old Gam didn't want to go back again. He told her how grateful Old Gam was and tried to return the seventy dollars, but Ah Heung wouldn't accept them. Instead, she insisted that Daksing take Old Gam once more to see the doctor. Dasking had no choice but to do as Ah Heung told him and accompanied Old Gam to the doctor for a second time. Old Gam got another injection, had some more medicine prescribed, and paid another thirty dollars.

Soon, Old Gam recovered. He cobbled together a hundred dollars by borrowing some from Daksing and Zyunfuk. He planned to return the money to Ah Heung when she came over. Ah Heung, however, did not accept it. She said she wanted Old Gam to use the money to buy some supplements. When Old Gam saw how sincere she was, he did not insist. But one day, he casually asked for her shoe size and in secret began to make a pair of leather shoes for her that he planned to give her as soon as they were finished.

As a result of this episode, Ah Heung was held even dearer by Old Gam, Daksing, and Zyunfuk. She was often on their minds, and when they did not see her for a couple of days, they'd miss her. When Ah Heung came over, there was always a lot to talk about. Later on, Ah Heung also joined in when Daksing and Zyunfuk bet on dogs and horses. What's more, she placed much larger bets than the two of them. Whenever she won, she treated everyone to tea and snacks. Sometimes Zyunfuk lost his entire stake, and Ah Heung would put up some more money for him. If he won, she would only take back the initial sum; but if he did not win, Ah Heung would not mention it anymore. Zyunfuk would of course be embarrassed, and a few days later when he had some money he naturally would want to return it, but by then Ah Heung herself would no longer remember. Sometimes she would even say he had already returned it to her and had gotten mixed up. Even though Ah Heung was determined to marry someone rich, she was never condescending toward her poor friends. The three of them marveled at her. Zyunfuk likened her to a fairy, Daksing compared her to a cool breeze on a hot day, and Old Gam who had watched Disney's *Snow White* said she was his Snow White.

A few months went by like this. Then, one day, Ah Heung brought over a letter, which she asked Zyunfuk to deliver to a hotel in Kowloon. She gave him ten dollars, which he did not want to accept, but Ah Heung said that the money came from her mistress and that there was no reason not to accept it. Zyunfuk went to deliver the letter. The recipient was an overseas Chinese from the Philippines. He asked Zyunfuk to wait for a while and wrote a reply, which he then passed to Zyunfuk. He also gave him another ten dollars. Zyunfuk brought back the letter and Ah Heung came to pick it up. The following day, she asked Zyunfuk to deliver another letter, and once more he came back with a reply.

Then, three days later at around eight thirty in the morning, when neither Zyunfuk nor Daksing had yet set up their stalls, Ah Heung suddenly came over and asked Old Gam to help her move two suitcases. Old Gam went to help Ah Heung bring the luggage to the entrance of Gousing Road. Then, Ah Heung hailed a cab.

"Your mistress wants to go on a trip?" he asked.

"I don't know, but she asked me to take these some place."

Old Gam helped Ah Heung put the suitcases into the trunk. Then she got into the cab, thanked him, and off she went.

V

At first Old Gam didn't notice, but eventually he realized that he hadn't seen Ah Heung for a couple of days. When they all started to be concerned, Old Gam told them what had happened that morning when he had seen her off.

The three of them began guessing what might have

happened. Zyunfuk said, "I am sure it's that Chinese-Filipino. She ran away with him. First, I delivered their letters, and then she brought over her luggage."

"I never once heard her say that she had any Chinese-Filipino friends," Daksing said, "and besides, that letter did not seem to be written by her."

"And judging by the suitcases," Old Gam observed, "they did not seem to belong to Ah Heung. They were fancy leather suitcases, which is why I asked her whether her mistress was going on a trip. She said that her mistress had asked her to take them some place."

"So why hasn't she come back?"

"Could she have fallen ill?"

"If she had fallen ill, she would have gone to see a doctor, and we would have seen her."

...

They debated back and forth for a long time but could not settle on an explanation that they all found convincing. At first they thought that sooner or later, Ah Heung would show up again, but then another two days passed and there still was no sign of her. Finally, they decided that they should buy some fruits and pastries and have Zyunfuk deliver them to the Si residence the following day. If she was there, then there'd be no problem, but if she wasn't there, he could just say that he was a relative from Canton who had come to see her and leave them for her.

Early the next morning, Zyunfuk went over to the Si residence. He rang the doorbell, and a healthy-looking older women who must have been in her sixties opened the door. When he inquired after Ah Heung, she told him that Ah Heung was her granddaughter and that she had gone to Macau the day before yesterday to get married. Zyunfuk originally had wanted to say that he had come from Guangdong province, but when that old lady said that she herself had just come over from Canton a few days ago, he changed his plan. He said that a certain Mr. Gam had asked him to deliver these snacks. He had wanted to ask the old lady some more questions, but she had already shut the door on him.

Upon his return, Zyunfuk reported everything to Old Gam and Daksing. They all felt even more perplexed. If Ah Heung had gotten married, then it must have been to that Chinese-Filipino. But why had her grandmother come out to Hong Kong? They then guessed that Ah Heung would probably move to the Philippines after her wedding and therefore had wanted her grandmother to come to Hong Kong so that they could spend some time together. That of course made complete sense.

Now that Ah Heung had found a good match, they naturally were happy for her. Nevertheless, they couldn't help but feel a little disappointed that she hadn't shared the news with her friends first. With Ah Heung gone, the three of them felt a little lonely, but otherwise everything was just as it had always been. Old Gam kept himself busy with his work, and whenever Daksing and Zyunfuk had nothing to do, they'd play chess. In this way, six days passed.

On the seventh day, just when Daksing had stepped into the street to buy something, he saw a car stop ahead of him. The person stepping out of the car was none other than Ah Heung! Her appearance had changed completely. She wore a green dress and high heels and had permed her hair. She had a diamond ring on one of her fingers and a shiny watch on her wrist. Daksing at first did not believe his eyes, but when Ah Heung turned her head to beckon the person in the car, he clearly saw that it was her. Daksing had assumed that the person stepping out of the car with her would be the Filipino-Chinese, but it actually turned out to be her master, Mr. Si. Daksing refrained from going over to greet them. Instead, he looked on as Mr. Si got out of the car and the two of them disappeared inside the residence. Only then did he run back to tell Old Gam and Zyunfuk.

"And you are sure you are not mistaken?" Old Gam asked.

"How can I be mistaken, I was standing right there and saw her go inside with her master."

"Just the two of them? What about that Filipino-Chinese?" Zyunfuk asked curiously.

"There were just the two of them," Daksing replied.

"I am sure that Mr. Si was their witness and now he has come back from Macau. Ah Heung is accompanying him and is meeting her grandmother at the same time," Old Gam said with certainty.

"Now that she has come back, I am sure she will come and see us," Daksing said.

"If she doesn't come, I am going over there again to see her," Zyunfuk said.

"Maybe she does not want us to come and see her," Old Gam said, considerate as ever.

"I'd say, best not to rush things. Let's wait a few days and see."

But then, early the next day, less than twenty-four hours after the three of them had discussed the matter, Ah Heung came to see them. She also brought a lot of things to eat. Some were for Old Gam, she said, and some for Daksing, and the rest for Zyunfuk. Without paying attention to Ah Heung's gifts, Old Gam straight out asked her why she had gotten married all of a sudden.

"And what about your husband? Who is he?" Daksing wanted to know.

"It's my master," Ah Heung said.

"Your master? That Mr. Si?" Zyunfuk asked in astonishment.

"Why not? He's rich, I like him; what's wrong with it?" Ah Heung replied candidly.

"So you will be his third wife!" Zyunfuk exclaimed, full of pity for Ah Heung.

"I guess," Ah Heung replied. "My mistress, that Ms. Si, she's left."

"She's left? And she won't be coming back?" Old Gam asked.

"She left with her Filipino-Chinese lover."

"Is he the one you had asked me to deliver a letter to the other day?" Zyunfuk asked.

"Yes, that was him. He is a soccer star in the Philippines. A few years ago, he went to Taipei and fell in love with my mistress. This time he came to Hong Kong. After the two had exchanged a few letters and seen each other once, my mistress decided to go off with him. But because she was afraid Mr. Si would be heartbroken, she asked me to take care of him. And now we got married."

"Are you sure you'll be happy that way?" Zyunfuk asked.

"Why not? I can have everything now."

"And we all thought you had gotten married to that Filipino-Chinese," Old Gam said.

"You guys really have a vivid imagination," Ah Heung said with a cheerful laugh.

"I am still somewhat puzzled, how rich is that Mr. Si really?" Old Gam asked.

"I am not entirely sure either," Ah Heung replied, "but I told him that while I don't have a lover, I have a lot of poor friends to look after, and three of them are right here in Gousing Road. And so Mr. Si said that he wants to give each of you a small shop in a newly built high rise in Kowloon. He wants you to open a business over there, so that you'll no longer be keeping an eye on him day in and day out over here."

"Really? How did all that come about?"

"Well, I asked him to lend a hand to my poor friends." Ah Heung laughed and took her leave. But Old Gam asked her to hold on. He took out something wrapped in paper from inside his stall, and said, "Just a little something, please don't laugh at me for not having done a better job with them."

Ah Heung tore open the wrapping and exclaimed, "Ah, a pair of leather shoes! Thank you!" She wrapped up the shoes again and went back, holding them tightly in her hands.

VI

Two weeks later, a big change came to Gousing Road.

The shoe repair stall was still there, but it was now run by a young cobbler who had taken over the lease from Old Gam. The hardware stall was gone, and the stall for potted flowers was now a fruit stall. On Nathan Road in Kowloon, a row of shops opened for business in a newly built high rise. Three of them were clustered together, and they had all moved over from Gousing Road.

One of them was "Old Gam's Leather Shoes."

The next was "Daksing's Metallurgy."

And the last one was "Zyunfuk All Lucky Electrical."

AFTERWORD
A Chinese Romantic's Journey through Time and Space: Xu Xu and Transnational Chinese Romanticism

I changed from one job to the next, and drifted from
place to place [...]. I sold my songs and my stories and
everything else to make ends meet. And in the end, I
drifted to Hong Kong. (Xu 2008, 6:406)

This is how the first-person narrator of Xu Xu's 徐訏 short story
"Bird Talk" 鳥語 (1951) ends up stranded in Hong Kong. He
arrives alone, the reader later learns, without his fiancée Yunqian,
who has stayed behind in mainland China. "Bird Talk" was
among the first works of fiction that Xu Xu (1908–80) wrote in
Hong Kong after leaving Shanghai in 1950 in the wake of the
founding of the People's Republic. Like many other mainland
émigrés, Xu Xu initially believed that his stay in Hong Kong
would be a temporary exile. In Shanghai, he left behind his wife
whom he had married the previous year and a two-month-old
daughter. Xu Xu's exile would last three decades and only came
to an end when he passed away in the Ruttonjee Hospital in

Wan Chai on Hong Kong Island on October 5, 1980, without ever having returned to China. Like the lonely narrator in "Bird Talk," Xu Xu reluctantly had to make Hong Kong his new home.

Nostalgia and a yearning for the lost homeland constitutes, according to Wolfgang Kubin, the defining characteristic of postwar diasporic literature in Chinese (Kubin 2005, 259–67). This literary phenomenon is particularly visible in Hong Kong's postwar literature, most of which was produced by writers who had sought exile in the British colony after leaving the newly founded People's Republic of China (PRC) and who are collectively referred to as "writers who came south" 南來作家. To Lo Wai-luen, the expression of a deeply felt sense of homesickness 滿懷的鄉思 thus became central not only to the creative work of Xu Xu but also to many of his contemporaries in Hong Kong, such as Sima Changfeng 司馬長風 and Li Huiying 李輝英, who both came to Hong Kong in 1949 and 1950 respectively (Lo 1998, 118–19). Nostalgia and homesickness also became a defining feature in the poetry of émigré writers like Li Kuang 力匡 and Zhao Zifan 趙滋蕃, as well as of Xu Xu, who, besides writing fiction, published several volumes of poetry in Hong Kong (Leung 2009, 24; Chan 2009, 52).

Nostalgia and homesickness as expressed in the works of these émigré writers, these critics argue, are inevitably tied up to the physical condition of exile in Hong Kong. To them, nostalgia was the catharsis through which these writers could express the pain of having had to leave their homes in mainland China and through which their pain could be made tangible for readers who shared a similar fate. Svetlana Boym calls this practice "restorative nostalgia," namely, a process through which an exile attempts to rebuild a lost home and patch up memory gaps (Boym 2002, 41–48).

Physical exile certainly was a painful reality for Xu Xu. Restorative nostalgia might to some extent have informed his literary activity in those years. However, nostalgia in Xu Xu's postwar fiction above all constitutes the expression of a quest for a purely aesthetic utopia that had already begun to take shape in his prewar oeuvre and that came to full fruition in his postwar fiction. This is particularly evident in his short stories from Hong Kong, such as "Bird Talk" and "The All-Souls Tree" 百靈樹 (1950), both of which are included in this anthology, and also in his novella *The Other Shore* 彼岸 (1951) that is discussed below.

Nostalgia in Xu Xu's fiction is ultimately time and place unspecific, and Xu Xu himself was aware of the limits and fallacy of restorative nostalgia. Instead, nostalgia was a way for Xu Xu to give expression both to a real sense of loss as well as to a sense of metaphysical homelessness that did not directly result from his exile in Hong Kong but that is as much bound up with the experience of modernity as it is with the reality of the new postwar world order.

Nostalgia thus becomes the expression of a literary aesthetic that connects Xu Xu to a number of other writers who are typically associated with a twentieth-century revival of romanticism, foremost among them Hermann Hesse (1877–1962). As it was for Xu Xu, the expression of nostalgia for Hesse was as much an aesthetic gesture as it was a political gesture. My understanding of Xu Xu's use of nostalgia thus challenges conventional interpretations of the use of nostalgia in postwar Chinese literature and enhances our understanding of the interplay of aesthetics and politics in the work of Chinese writers in exile.

The French-Brazilian philosopher Michael Löwy understands the romantic critique of modernity as bound up with an experience of loss:

> The Romantic vision is characterized by the painful and melancholic conviction that in the modern reality something precious has been lost, at the level of both individuals and humanity at large; certain essential human values have been alienated. This alienation, keenly

sensed, is often experienced as exile [...]. (Löwy 2001, 21)

Löwy quotes Friedrich Schlegel as speaking of the soul, the seat of humanness, as living "under the willows of exile [unter den Trauerweiden der Verbannung]," far removed from the true hearth of homeland (Löwy 2001, 21). It is precisely this sense of metaphysical homelessness, I believe, that lies at the root of the nostalgic longing expressed by Xu Xu's fictional protagonists.

Löwy's study on romanticism informs my own reading of Xu Xu in another way. Löwy understands romanticism as a highly diverse movement whose numerous strands can be found in genres and literatures not usually thought to be part of the romantic canon. By drawing on Xu Xu's own critical writing on the role of the artist in society and by illustrating his intellectual proximity to writers and thinkers of the romantic movement, I will argue here that Xu Xu's postwar fiction contributes to a transnational romantic canon and constitutes a creative engagement with romantic aesthetics that links modern Chinese literature to a global literary modernity.

Xu Xu's literary oeuvre has been linked to post- or neo-romanticism ever since his "rediscovery" by mainland scholars in the 1980s (Yan 1986 and 1989; Geng 2004).[1] Yan Jiayan was among the first to describe Xu Xu's prewar work as "brimming with the hue of romanticism," emphasizing Xu Xu's tendency to create fantastic plots in exoticized settings and his fascination with romance (Yan 1989, 309). Yan's categorization of Xu Xu as a "post-romantic" appears to follow the logic that Xu Xu's work appeared chronologically after those of an earlier group of Chinese writers active in the 1920s who are typically referred to as "romantics." These writers, who include Guo Moruo 郭沫若 (1892-1978), Tian Han 田漢 (1898-1968), and Yu Dafu 郁達夫 (1896-1945), after coming into contact with the works of European romantics such as Goethe, Coleridge, and Lord Byron while studying abroad in Europe or Japan, had begun to emulate (at least temporarily) the celebration of nature, sublime love, subjectivism, and idealism typical of nineteenth-century European romantic literature.

It was thus primarily the ubiquitousness of certain "romantic" sensibilities and characteristics as displayed by these early-twentieth-century writers that led Yan and other scholars—including Leo Lee in his seminal study of Chinese romanticism (Lee 1973)—to place the works of Yu Dafu and Xu Xu into the romantic canon. Less of a factor was the question of whether they constituted a "genuine Chinese romanticism" that developed as a conscious or unconscious literary response to certain sociocultural phenomena, in the way European romanticism is usually understood as a reaction to French Enlightenment ideals and the Industrial Revolution (Safransky 2007; Berlin 1999).

The term "neo-romanticism" is itself not unproblematic. In the West, it has—at least since the 1930s—been used to describe all movements after around 1890 that countered Naturalism (Kimmich 1937, 126–37; Schwede 1987, 26–36). Simultaneously, it has been linked to the effects of mechanization and mass warfare, especially in twentieth-century Europe. Characterized by a boundless subjectivism and a turning away from the present, neo-romantic works of literature were believed to excessively celebrate aestheticism, ignore ethical concerns, and portray an overreaching and isolating individualism. Particularly manifest in poetry, neo-romanticism celebrated exotic locales, like Renaissance Italy, and displayed an interest in myths, sagas, and the marvelous. It was linked to French Symbolism but also to the aesthetics of the Art Nouveau movements and Impressionism.

Stefan George, himself considered a representative of neo-romanticism, was credited with defining a loose canon of neo-romantic poets through his anthology of European verse termed *Contemporary Poetry* (Zeitgenössische Dichtung) from

1913, which included poems by Swinburne, Dowson, Koos, Verlaine, Mallarmé, Rimbaud, and others.

In fiction, both an individual's search for a unique spiritual and physical identity amidst the backdrops of nature and modern civilization as well as the role of art in the formation of personal identity are seen as intrinsic to the neo-romantic sensitivity. The turn-of-the century works of Gerhart Hauptmann, the brothers Heinrich and Thomas Mann, and Hermann Hesse, through their aesthetic escapism and exoticism, are usually ascribed neo-romantic tendencies.

Xu Xu himself was acutely aware of these literary phenomena, and he frequently commented on them in his critical essays, some of which will be discussed below. At the same time, his literary works not only shared some of the aesthetic concerns of his romantic and neo-romantic predecessors and contemporaries but, more importantly, were born out of similar sociopolitical concerns and responded to similar sociocultural phenomena. It is for this reason, I will illustrate, that Xu Xu's work needs to be read within the context of what I call "transnational romanticism."

* * *

Unlike the fictional protagonist in "Bird Talk," Xu Xu arrived in Hong Kong as a literary celebrity. According to Murong Yujun, Xu Xu's readers would frequently track him down at the Gloucester Café in Causeway Bay, clasping copies of his books and asking him for a signature (Murong 2003, 15). Xu Xu had been one of the most popular writers of the Republican period. He had shot to stardom in prewar Shanghai with exotic romances such as "Goddess of the Arabian Sea" 阿拉伯海的女神 (1936) and "Ghost Love" 鬼戀 (1937), stories in which confident and modern urban first-person narrators fall in love with mysterious women who invariably challenge the narrator's professed rationality.

Many of these were at least in part inspired by Xu Xu's sojourn in Europe. Xu Xu had embarked on study abroad in Paris in 1936 but had returned to Shanghai after the outbreak of war with Japan the following year. Xu Xu eventually left Shanghai in 1942, not long after the foreign concessions had been occupied by Japan, and relocated to Chongqing, the Nationalist government's wartime capital. In Chongqing, Xu Xu's epic spy-romance *The Rustling Wind* 風蕭蕭 (1942), set in occupied Shanghai, was serialized to great acclaim in the wartime paper *Eradicator Daily* 掃蕩報. Xu Xu briefly returned to Shanghai in 1946 and with the help of Liu Yichang 劉以鬯 (1918–2018) began to publish his wartime works, many of which had previously only appeared in journals or newspapers (Liu 2002a, 208). These books met with great success: *The Rustling Wind* went through three printruns in less than a year and "Ghost Love" through nineteen by the end of 1949.[2]

Yet while the reading public was fond of Xu Xu's exotic first-person narratives that frequently challenged conventional perceptions of reality, the leftist literary establishment had long been critical of Xu Xu's fictional output. In 1938, the influential Marxist critic Ba Ren 巴人, the pen name of Wang Renshu 王任叔 (1901–72), had called Xu Xu's fiction "a bomb full of poison," capable of "extinguishing the fighting spirit of thousands of revolutionaries" (Wang 1995, 65–67), while in 1945 Shi Huaichi 石懷池 (1925–45?), another leftist critic, had urged readers "not to read Xu Xu's books anymore […] and to throw them into the cesspool" (Shi 1945, 151–54).[3] Once the Communist Party had assumed power in China and established the People's Republic, it did not take long for Xu Xu to realize that his prewar literary legacy would invariably turn out to be a considerable liability, and he decided to temporarily relocate to Hong Kong.

What both Ba Ren and Shi Huaichi had taken issue with was Xu Xu's obvious rejection of and opposition to the social-realist mode of narration that the literary left had been promoting in earnest, especially after the founding of the League of Leftist Writers 中國左翼作家聯盟 in 1930. While progressive writers like Lu Xun 魯迅 (1881–1936) or critics like Ba Ren believed that literature played an important role in the struggle for social renewal, Xu Xu's fiction, Shi Huaichi argued, would invariably cause the reader to "distance [oneself] from that cruel struggle between old and new that is currently being carried out all around us […]" and instead "invite [one] to enter an illusionary world" (Shi 1945, 153).

Xu Xu would not have disagreed with the charge. In fact, he had frequently displayed his overt preference for the aesthetic value of illusion over realist methods in his fiction. In "The Goddess of the Arabian Sea," for example, the protagonist who falls in love with a mysterious woman on board a steamer to Europe at one point declares, "I want to pursue all artistic fantasies, because their beauty to me is reality," and then announces that "in this world there are people who pursue dreams of the real 求真實的夢, while I seek out the real within dreams 求夢的真實" (Xu 2008, 5:219).

Xu Xu's insistence on the artistic value of illusions resonates with Bergsonian concepts of intuition that he had become interested in while studying at Peking University in the late 1920s (Green 2011: 89-90). Henri Bergson (1859-1941), a philosopher who himself is considered an heir to the romantic movement and who had a major impact on European modernists such as Proust, Virginia Woolf, and T. S. Eliot, appealed to the artist to seek for truths and realities beyond the purely mimetic. Like Schelling before him, who saw in the aesthetic act the highest act of reason, Bergson believed that the artist had an intuitive ability to enter into immediate communication with an object, with nature, and with the self.

The belief in art's ability to grant access to truths and realities defiant of scientific reason and customarily hidden by our everyday experiences greatly appealed to Xu Xu, and he frequently explored it in his fiction. In his 1947 short story

"Hallucination" 幻覺, for example, the story's narrator meets a painter who, whenever he gazes at one of his small oil paintings, is able to access his own past and temporarily relive the happiness he knew with his now deceased lover. He further claims to briefly unite with her once a day when she appears as an apparition at sunrise, and he proclaims to the incredulous narrator that "illusions and reality are very difficult to tell apart, for reality may consist of the common illusions of the majority, while an illusion can be one person'zs reality" (Xu 2008, 5:72).

* * *

The question of what constituted the appropriate way to depict reality remained a highly contested topic in the newly founded PRC. While progressive Chinese writers of the 1920s and 1930s had embraced literary realism that was largely inspired by the works of Dostoevsky, Zola, and Dickens and that was concerned with making visible the societal deficiencies of Republican-period China, Soviet-style socialist realism eventually became the only officially sanctioned art form in the PRC. Declared the new artistic orthodoxy by Mao Zedong in his famous 1942 speech at the Yan'an Forum for Literature and Arts, socialist realism had been introduced to China a few years earlier by the Marxist critic Zhou Yang 周揚 (1908–89), who in 1936 had laid the theoretical foundation for its implementation in his essay "Thoughts on Realism" 現實主義試論. Pointing out the indisputable correlation between political art and political doctrine, Zhou Yang stated that the

> [n]ew realist methods must be based on a correct modern worldview. A correct worldview can guarantee true understanding of the laws of social development […]; it can also greatly enhance the ideological force of artistic creation. (Zhou 1996, 339)

Even in his Hong Kong exile, Xu Xu remained invested in the question of what constituted the appropriate artistic approach to depicting reality. At the same time, he was highly critical of the politicization of literature and art in the PRC and frequently commented on the new literary climate that prevailed in China. In an essay from 1954 entitled "Some Thoughts on Realism" 從寫實主義談起, Xu Xu writes that realism in the West originally had come about in the nineteenth century as a reaction to romanticism and that it corresponded to the rise of positivism and materialism in philosophy (Xu 2008, 10:145). Its prominence in the arts began to wane, Xu Xu continues, in the late nineteenth century with the onset of modern psychology, especially Freudianism, which in philosophy gave rise to a new interest in idealism. To Xu Xu, the various contemporary artistic currents, such as "surrealism, symbolism, neo-romanticism, and existentialism all came about as a reaction to realism" because "humans have a desire for their own minds to explore dreams and illusions in order to obtain a deeper understanding of reality" (Xu 2008, 10:145). This is because "among the totality of reality a person can grasp, there is nothing like the reality that can be engaged with in one's mind. Even the external world examined by an individual is nothing but the impressions and experiences that exist in one individual's mind" (Xu 2008, 10:145).

Xu Xu then points out that in the Soviet Union and the countries behind the Iron Curtain, realism in the form of "new realism" 新現實主義 or "scientific realism" 科學現實主義 has become inseparable from politics, because it is now meant to reflect political reality and to promote politics. However, for Xu Xu, "the mission of literature and art lies beyond the realm of politics" (Xu 2008, 10:147). He personally has nothing against individuals who choose "to walk the old road of realism" 走寫實主義的舊路, Xu Xu concludes, it is just that "I personally feel that realism cannot satisfy me" (Xu 2008, 10:147).

While Xu Xu's criticism in "Some Thoughts on Realism"

was clearly aimed at the state of literature in mainland China, it is important to note that Xu Xu was equally critical of the politicization of literature in Taiwan and Hong Kong. Anti-Communism, whether aimed at the PRC or at the Soviet Union, as Michelle Yeh reminds us, was a major component of postwar cultural policy in the Taiwan of Chiang Kai-shek 蔣介石 (1887-1975) (Yeh 2007, 120). Hong Kong, on the other hand, had been given an important role in America's campaign of psychological warfare against the PRC. The United States Information Service (USIS) in Hong Kong came to sponsor a great deal of literature—known as Greenback Culture 綠背文化—that denounced the new regime. Lu Yishi 路易士 was a prominent writer and poet who frequently wrote for journals supported by the USIS, and Eileen Zhang 張愛玲 wrote her novel *The Rice-Sprout Song* (1955) about the land reform in Communist China under their commission.[4]

Xu Xu had left Shanghai in 1950 for political reasons, and he remained an outspoken critic of the CCP's cultural policies throughout his exile in Hong Kong. However, his indictment of the promotion of anti-Communist propaganda in both Taiwan and Hong Kong was equally scathing. In an essay from 1955 he wrote that

> [m]uch of Taiwan's literature is anti-Communist 反共, but in an immature way. In fact, there is likewise a lot of anti-Communist literature from Hong Kong and South Asia, but it is all equally lacking and immature. And what makes an intelligent person feel astonished is that the more this literature gets promoted the worse it gets and the more it resembles the conceptualized and formalized literature of the mainland. (Xu 1991, 275)

* * *

Free from the limitations of state-prescribed socialist real-ism in the PRC or the proto-fascist policies toward artistic expression of the KMT in Taiwan, Xu Xu in his early Hong Kong fiction continued to engage with Bergsonian phenome-nology while also exploring new topical and aesthetic concerns. His short story "Bird Talk," written shortly after he arrived in Hong Kong and serialized in the literary supplement of the *Sing Tao Evening Post* 星島晚報, perfectly embodies his aesthetic vision from those years. The narrator of "Bird Talk" is similar to the first-person narrators who populated much of his prewar fiction in that he shares elements of Xu Xu's biography and nar-rates a personal experience that largely defies rational explana-tion. The setting of the story in prewar rural China and Shanghai and the exploration of nostalgia and homelessness, on the other hand, would become the hallmark of Xu Xu's fictional oeuvre from Hong Kong.

"Bird Talk" opens with the narrator receiving a worn copy of the Diamond Sutra and a letter that informs him of the death of a certain nun named Juening 覺寧 (Peaceful Awareness). The letter greatly saddens the narrator and evokes in him memories of China from before his exile in Hong Kong.

It is the account of these memories that is narrated as a long flashback and constitutes the main body of "Bird Talk." Once the flashback gets under way the reader learns that because the narrator is suffering from a bout of depression he had decided to leave Shanghai temporarily to convalesce in the countryside. While staying with his grandmother in his ancestral village, he encounters Yunqian, a shy and introverted young woman whose autistic features cause the villagers to slight her. The narrator, however, is drawn to her mysterious charm, especially after he witnesses one morning that she appears to be able to communi-cate with birds:

It was a hazy morning. The sky was colorless except for a faint red glow in the east. Soon, the birds in the bamboo thicket started to sing. […] Just then, I heard a response from beyond the fence and I caught sight of the girl, wearing a gray dress, her hair done up in two braids. A chorus of birds began chirping from inside the bamboo thicket. […] The girl raised her head. Her face was round, and her eyes shone brightly. She bore a happy smile. The sounds she was making were beautiful. They neither sounded like the trilling of birds, nor did they sound like singing. The girl and the two birds seemed like old acquaintances. (Xu 2008, 6:375)

Intrigued by her unusual talent, the narrator offers to school Yunqian in math and Chinese, hoping that she might teach him bird talk in return. Yunqian, however, is just as unreceptive to modern schooling as the narrator is incapable of learning bird talk. However, when one day she happens to come across a poem the narrator had written the previous day, she expresses an instant liking for it, and the narrator realizes that despite her limited literacy, she is highly susceptible to poetry. The two start to read Tang poetry, the meaning and beauty of which Yunqian seems to grasp intuitively. When the narrator has to return to Shanghai, he decides to take Yunqian with him. However, in the bustling modern city, she is deeply unhappy and reverts to her shy and introverted self. When she eventually begs the narrator to let her return home, he decides to abandon his own life in the city and to live with Yunqian in the countryside. On their way back to their ancestral village where they plan to get married, they overnight in a small nunnery. In the nunnery, Yunqian is introduced to the Diamond Sutra and displays the same intuitive understanding as when she had first encountered poetry. This then prompts the narrator to leave her in the nunnery and return to Shanghai alone:

I knew well that Yunqian was detached from such
yearnings and that she was of a nobler kind. She did not
belong with me; she belonged in a world unspoiled by
worldly matters. Only in such a world could her sublimity and magnificence manifest itself. Only in such
a world could she truly feel at ease and be happy. (Xu
2008, 6:405)

Back in Shanghai, the narrator leads a meaningless life full
of sin and regret until, years later, he "eventually drifted to Hong
Kong" (Xu 2008, 6:406). It is here where he receives the news of
the passing of Yunqian, who had changed her name to Juening
after her ordination. The novel ends with a line from the Diamond Sutra, read out under tears by the narrator: "All sentient
beings [...] will eventually be led by me to enter Nirvana where
all their anguish will be extinguished" (Xu 2008, 6:407).

"Bird Talk" epitomizes Xu Xu's view of the function and
role of art in society. Yunqian has an intuitive ability to appre-
ciate art and Buddhist sutras in a sensually cognitive way that
enlarges her consciousness. In addition, her unusual gift to
communicate with birds makes her part of the sublime spheres
of nature and the universe. It was access to such spheres that
romantics like Schelling (and Bergson a century later) believed
the genuine work of art might enable. Xu Xu, in what reads like
a genuine act of romantic irony, at first reverses this process in
that Yunqian, who already possesses a transcendental self-con-
sciousness because of her ability to communicate with birds,
gains access to the conventional world of man—of education
and socialization—by way of the very means that are thought to
transport man away from normality: art, or, in this case, poetry.
Xu Xu's use of irony here reminds us of Lu Xun's novella *The
Diary of a Madman* 狂人日記 (1918). It is only in what appears
to society as a state of mental confusion or madness that the protagonist is able to gain true understanding of the cannibalistic
and self-destructive nature of China's society.

Yet Xu Xu's use of irony differs from that of Lu Xun in a fundamental way. While Lu Xun clearly laments China's national deficiency, the root of which he sees planted in centuries of Confucian socialization, Xu Xu's lament is that of modern man, indicting not Chinese society, or society at large, but modern man's inability to be one with nature and to see beyond the scientifically proven and socially accepted. Lu Xun is not nostalgic. On the contrary, his plea to "save the children" at the end of his novel is clearly directed toward a utopian future.

Xu Xu's quote from the Diamond Sutra also terminates "Bird Talk" on a utopian note. Yet while Yunqian, as the reader is made to infer, might have reached nirvana, the narrator, who through her gained a glimpse of its attainability, remains behind in Hong Kong, a city he now reluctantly calls home. Only when he leaves the city and ventures into the mountains (presumably the then still largely undeveloped New Territories) is his mind transported back to a lost paradise that is no less utopian:

> Every time I travel to the countryside and gaze at the
> mountains and streams and the lush forests, and I
> hear the distant singing of birds, the figure of Yunqian
> flashes into my memory. (Xu 2008, 6:406)

The Hong Kong scholar Wang Pu has described Xu Xu's fictional reminiscences and his celebration of the pastoral beauty of his childhood home that we see in "Bird Talk" and several other of his Hong Kong stories as the expression of his nostalgia for his lost home, or, as she puts it, the "elegiac mourning for a pastoral of former days" 田園牧歌式往日的傷悼 (Wang 2003, 101). Another example of this can be found in Xu Xu's short story "Elopement" 私奔 (1951, translated as "Sister Tsui-ling" by George Kao 喬志高 [1912–2008]) that consists of a first-person narrator's reminiscences of his childhood in Fengyang village, an idyllic place where he used to roam the fields with his friends, had a childhood crush on the lovable and beautiful Cuiling, and was saved from a drifting sampan by the heroic Zhiming. It is with Zhiming that Cuiling eventually eloped, to avoid an arranged marriage, a plan that she only shared with the narrator, whom she called her little brother. Cuiling and Zhiming eventually end up in Shanghai where the narrator meets them one day several years later, only to notice to his great dismay that the idols of his youth had become frighteningly ordinary members of the urban bourgeoisie. "All the beautiful images which had projected themselves in my child's mind," he soberly concludes, "disappeared in the face of reality" (Xu 1974, 113).

Both "Bird Talk" and "Elopement" clearly idealize rural China of the Republican era and are expressions of the kind of nostalgia for a bygone era and a lost home that characterizes much of Hong Kong postwar fiction by émigré writers. At the same time, both stories embody a kind of nostalgia that Michael Löwy believes to be at the center of all romantic nostalgia, namely the nostalgia or longing for an idealized pre-capitalist past where the past becomes the locus onto which the narrator's longing is directed, a homeland to which Schlegel's exiled soul could return but which in its pastoral beauty might never have existed in the first place. Löwy argues that

> [t]his Romantic restitutionism may indeed be deemed the most important of all, from both the qualitative and quantitative viewpoint [...]. It is the closest to the essence of the overall phenomenon [of Romanticism], given that nostalgia for a pre-capitalist state lies at the heart of this worldview. (Löwy 2001, 59)

According to Löwy, it finds articulation in the writing of romantics such as Novalis and Coleridge and also in the neo-romantic work of Gottfried Ben and Julius Evola, both of whom expressed in their work "their hatred of the modern world in its bourgeois, capitalist, urban, scientific ... aspects" and their "dreams of a primitive past of instinctual life" (Löwy 2001, 68).

Xu Xu himself observed this tendency of certain twentieth-century modernists to articulate in their works a skepticism toward the limits of scientific progress, radical finalism, and mechanism. In his 1954 essay entitled "A Hard-born Era" 難產時代, Xu Xu writes that

> [f]ollowing World War One, artistic and intellectual culture underwent tremendous changes. The promises of the nineteenth century of a mechanized civilization and the foundations that had been believed to be unshakable all started to shake. The assumption that humankind had touched the cornerstone of progress suddenly began to lose its credibility after World War One. (Xu 2008, 10:161)

As a result, Xu Xu argues, literature lost its confidence in mankind. "The literature of the Twentieth Century," Xu Xu writes, "is a literature of 'doubt' 懷疑. All great writers began to explore in their souls worlds of gloom and terror, of mysticism and desperation" (Xu 2008, 10:162). This new literature, he continues, "no longer has any trust in the kind of reality produced by mankind" (Xu 2008, 10:162). In addition, Xu Xu notes that "under the illuminating effects of new developments in psychology, notions of what constitutes 'reality' 現實 and what constitutes subjective illusions 主觀的幻覺 have become increasingly difficult to separate" (Xu 2008, 10:162). Xu Xu then provides a list of some of the writers whom he considers masters of this new type of literature: "There are the Germans Hermann Hesse and Thomas Mann, the Frenchmen Marcel Proust and André Gide, the Englishmen James Joyce [sic] and T. S. Eliot, and the American Faulkner" (Xu 2008, 10:163).

Xu Xu's reference to Hermann Hesse (1877–1962) is particularly noteworthy here because of the many strikingly similar aesthetic concerns explored in their respective literary oeuvres. Hesse, one of the most prominent heirs of the romantic movement, had been awarded the Nobel Prize for Literature in 1946 while Xu Xu was in Washington as a correspondent for *Eradicator Daily*, the wartime paper that had serialized his novel *The Rustling Wind*. Xu Xu must have felt an artistic kinship with Hesse: Both had an apparent preference for first-person (and at times quasi-autobiographical) narrators, and both frequently made use of changing narrative perspectives that switched between first- and second-person narration. Both engaged in their work with mysticism, spirituality, and the surreal, and both celebrated in their fiction and poetry the sublimity of love. Furthermore, the image of the restless wanderer, epitomized in Hesse's iconic *Steppenwolf*, found its counterpart in many of Xu Xu's Hong Kong stories, such as in the disillusioned narrator in "Bird Talk," the lovesick wanderer in his novella *The Other Shore*, and the heartbroken narrator in the novel *Time and Brightness* 時與光 (1966) who likewise finds himself stranded in Hong Kong.

Especially *The Other Shore*, a tale about love found and lost, resembles some of Hesse's most famous works, such as *Siddhartha* (1922), Hesse's iconic tale about a spiritual journey of self-discovery.[5] The memory of harmony and beauty the narrator in *The Other Shore* once experienced while in love with Lulian, a nurse who saves him from suicide and whose own suicide is triggered by the narrator's betrayal of her, becomes the object of the narrator's nostalgia during a long stay at a lighthouse. There, a combination of quasi-religious epiphanies and the wisdom of an old lighthouse keeper give him a glimpse of hope of once more attaining the sublime state of bliss he had felt around Lulian. His experience somewhat mirrors that of Hesse's protagonist in *Siddhartha*, who comes to the realization that it is only through a totality of experiences that one can gain glimpses of understanding and who has a first taste of enlightenment while living with the wise ferryman Vasudeva by the river in which he had originally attempted to drown himself.

Both Hesse and Xu Xu displayed religious eclecticism in

their works, and while *Siddhartha* as well as *The Other Shore* and "Bird Talk" clearly carry Buddhist overtones, it is important to note that neither Hesse nor Xu Xu had much interest in the ritualistic aspect of religion or believed that any one religion could ultimately lead to salvation. Rather, each insisted that only through the overcoming of self could there be a return to or fusion with the origin of the universe.

If for the young Xu Xu, Europe and Western civilization had been a source of inspiration and longing, it was the East and its mysticism that had a particular appeal to Hesse. His *Journey to the East* (1932), for example, is told by a first-person narrator named H. H. who, together with a group of famous historical figures, embarks on a pilgrimage to the East in search of the ultimate Truth. Their journey, the narrator proclaims, "was not only mine and now; this procession of believers and disciples towards the Home of Light [...] was only a wave in the eternal striving of human beings, of the eternal strivings of the human spirit towards the East, towards Home" (Hesse 1956, 12–13). Their destination, then, is as nostalgic-utopian as the quest of the narrator in Xu Xu's *The Other Shore* or "Bird Talk."

In *Journey to the East*, Hesse appears to explore a phenomenon that Georg Steiner so aptly termed "nostalgia for the absolute" in his 1974 Massey lecture series of the same title. Steiner argues that it was the erosion of religious life in nineteenth- and twentieth-century Europe and the resulting moral and emotional vacuum that made humans seek out alternative mythologies such as Marxism, Freudian psychoanalysis, astrology, or new pseudo-religions. Nostalgia for the absolute, Steiner suggests, is "representative of the great current of thought and feeling in Europe we call romanticism" (Steiner 1997, 6). This metaphysical kind of nostalgia, Steiner writes, "was directly provoked by the decline of Western man and society, of the ancient and magnificent architecture of religious certitude. Like never before, today at this point in the twentieth century, we hunger for myths, for total explanation: we are starving for guaranteed prophecy" (Steiner 1997, 5-6). The nostalgia for a prelapsarian home that Hesse believes awaits the seeker in the East Steiner calls "Orientalism," arguing that it "is habitual to Western feeling from the time of the Greek mystery cults to Freemasonry and beyond" and that it "inspires the work of Hermann Hesse, of C. G. Jung, and, to some extent, of T. S. Eliot" (Steiner 1997, 44).

* * *

It is the same kind of nostalgia for the absolute, one is tempted to conclude, that Xu Xu displayed in his postwar fiction and that drove him to turn to the fantastic and surreal as an ultimate recourse for his protagonists' nostalgia. Xu Xu had already displayed an intense interest in the fantastic in his prewar fiction. In works like "The Goddess of the Arabian Sea" or "Ghost Love," Xu Xu used the fantastic as a literary device in order to appropriate modernist European literary techniques and aesthetics, Bergsonian phenomenology in particular, and to challenge the politicization of literature by mostly leftist writers (Green 2011, 68-69).

However, for the most part, the fantastic in Xu Xu's prewar fiction eventually was unmasked as merely uncanny encounters or else as dreams from which the narrator awoke in the end. Xu Xu's use of the fantastic in his postwar fiction from Hong Kong was of a different nature, as is evident in the two stories "The All-Souls Tree" and "Departed Soul" 離魂 (1964). In both, the embrace of the fantastic and the surreal as the driving plot element is a clear manifestation of an impulse Löwy identifies as the utopian projection of every romantic artistic creation: a world of beauty created by the imagination in the present (Löwy 2001, 23). If romantic writers in the West had discovered the fantastic as an artistic weapon against the constraints of reason dictated by enlightenment thinkers, as Löwy argues, twentieth-century surrealist writers in the West like André Breton discovered its appeal "as a secular alternative to the religious stranglehold on access to the universe of the non-rational" (Löwy 2001, 217).

In "The All-Souls Tree," a first-person narrator recounts his experience during a sojourn in Taiwan in the early 1950s. On a trip to Mount Ali, the narrator meets Xiancheng, a reticent young woman who had only recently relocated to Taiwan from China. One stormy night, the narrator notices how Xiancheng sneaks out of their hostel. He follows her and finds her standing greatly disturbed under an all-souls tree 百靈樹, insisting that the wailing sound of the wind in the tree crown is the wailing of her fiancé from whom she had been separated during the civil war on the mainland and who, she is certain, must have died. When a few days later, the narrator wants to pay Xiancheng a visit, he finds her home full of mourners. It turns out that Xiancheng committed suicide after receiving a telegram that informed her of her fiancé's death. He had died, we learn, on the night of the storm.

Even more pronounced is the evocation of the fantastic in "Departed Soul." A first-person narrator loses his wife not long after their marriage. Overcome by grief, he frequently dreams of her and often visits her grave, until he leaves Shanghai when it is occupied by the Japanese. After the war, he returns to Shanghai, where he starts a relationship with the singer Yuanxiang. When during an outing, they pass a wedding ceremony, the narrator suddenly has a flashback of his own wedding and causes a serious car accident in which Yuanxiang dies. The narrator himself falls into a coma during which he frequently encounters his former wife. Finally released from the hospital, the narrator decides to visit his wife's grave, and he encounters a young woman dressed in a gray gown who has an uncanny resemblance to his wife. Doubtful at first, he becomes convinced that she is in fact his former wife, especially after overhearing a conversation between her and an old woman in whose house they hide from a sudden rainstorm. But when he returns there after a few days, he finds the house abandoned, and is told by a farmer that the owner died many years ago. Yet when he looks back one last time, he sees "[…] just for a moment, […] the figure of the woman in the gray gown" (Xu 1971, 18).[6]

Unlike the fantastic in Xu Xu's prewar stories, the fantastic in his postwar fiction is no longer questioned by a supposedly enlightened narrator who needs to be convinced of its marvelous nature. Nor is the fantastic unmasked as the merely uncanny when the narrator awakes from a dream, as often happened at the end of his early stories. In both "The All-Souls Tree" and "Departed Soul," the fantastic event is witnessed and faithfully recounted by a narrator who passes no judgment on its probability.

While the use of the fantastic in these short stories clearly echoes Xu Xu's own aesthetic preferences discussed above, it also mirrors European twentieth-century artistic currents that embraced the fantastic, the mythical, and the surreal. As a literary movement, especially as articulated by André Breton, Surrealism claimed to take in the whole spectrum of human activity, "embracing hitherto neglected areas of life like dreams and the unconscious" (Ades 1994, 124). Its celebration of myths, Löwy further reminds us, facilitated the articulation of "the innermost emotion of human being […] in its haste to express itself" (Löwy 2001, 218).

Xu Xu likewise shared this preference for the mythical in literature and art, something he believed was largely lacking in modern Chinese literature. In an obituary for Lin Yutang 林語堂 (1895–1976), Xu Xu remembers how he had discussed this question with Lin, stating that writers and thinkers like Lu Xun, Zhou Zuoren, or Hu Shi all lacked a sense of mysticism 神祕感. In the West, Xu Xu continues, thinkers like Rousseau had also lacked it, while "Blaise Pascal and Henri Bergson both were imbued with plenty of mysticism" (Xu 2003, 81).

In twentieth-century painting, the impulse to incorporate the fantastic, the illogical, and poetic mythology is nowhere more apparent than in the work of Marc Chagall (1887–1985). Especially his dreamlike evocations of his childhood home in Belarus, characterized by scenes of pastoral beauty, joyful musicians, and blissful lovers hovering in a blue sky, invite the viewer to assume what Anne Goldman describes as an "angelic gaze" (Goldman 2008, 17). "Chagall paints dreams," she writes, "the language of space speaking for time, the high-flown perspectives of the canvases carrying us far away from the present" (Goldman 2008, 17). Like Xu Xu's fiction, Chagall's canvases are imbued with nostalgia, a nostalgia that, in the context of the Soviet Union's refusal to embrace Chagall, Goldman finds almost perplexing and touching.

Like Xu Xu, Chagall was an exile. Finding a home in France after the Russian Revolution and the First World War, he ends up as a refugee from the Holocaust in New York. Here, his beloved wife Bella passed away from an infection in 1944. Yet on his canvas, the past becomes the same light-filled prelapsarian Eden as Xu Xu's prewar childhood home in his Hong Kong stories. Chagall's natal Vitebsk was forever the place where he found sublime love, just as prewar Shanghai was for Xu Xu from his Hong Kong exile. Yet nostalgia in Chagall's paintings—just like the nostalgia found in Xu Xu's postwar fiction—is not the expression of a yearning for a concrete place or time. Instead, the past and the people and places that come alive in the dreamscapes captured on Chagall's warm and colorful canvases are artistic sanctuaries for his inner self.

Chagall himself rejected the use of the term "fantasy" to describe his work. "All our interior world is reality," he asserted in an interview from 1944, "and that perhaps more so than our apparent world. To call everything that appears illogical 'fantasy' […] would be practically to admit not understanding nature" (Chipp 1968: 440). Xu Xu must have sensed an artistic affinity to Chagall—how else can one explain that he chose to adorn the cover of his anthology *Step by Step, Mr. Everyman* 小人物的上進 (1964) that contained the story "Departed Soul" with Chagall's *Ciel d'Hiver (L'Accordéoniste)* (1942–50; see page 125), an oil painting that shows a young woman and young accordion player drifting through a wintry sky, high above a rural landscape?

In "The All-Souls Tree" and "Departed Soul," Xu Xu expressed his idealistic tendencies and his artistic belief that interior worlds shape external reality. Both stories also underscore Xu Xu's aesthetic preference for the use of nostalgia. However, as with "Bird Talk," nostalgia ultimately is place and time unspecific and is foremost the expression of the melancholic conviction that in the present reality something precious has been lost.

Xu Xu's physical exile in Hong Kong only partly explains the frequency with which nostalgia is invoked in his fiction. His celebration of the pastoral paradise of his childhood home and the use of the fantastic as a way to project interior worlds were as much political gestures in defiance of authoritarian policies regarding literature and art in China and Taiwan as they were the aesthetic gestures that connected him to a global romantic revival in the twentieth century. If romanticism is indeed a weltanschauung or worldview, as Michael Löwy asserts, that may be expressed in quite diverse cultural realms (Löwy 2001, 14), then Xu Xu's fiction clearly possesses the virtue of enabling the critic to "recognize the cultural multiplicity of romanticism" (Löwy 2001, 7).

To describe Xu Xu's aesthetics as a form of "transnational Chinese romanticism" is above all a heuristic gesture. Romanticism as a conceptual tool can help us discern the shared features and preoccupations of a set of twentieth-century texts that all respond to similar historical circumstances in similar fashion. It is through the lens of this redefined romanticism, then, that Xu Xu's oeuvre partakes in what Löwy describes as a highly diverse global literary modernity and that Xu Xu's readers were (and still are) able to find metaphysical sanctuaries from their mundane existence and the challenges of modern life.

Endnotes

1. Like the works of many other Republican-period writers, Xu Xu's works were unavailable to readers in mainland China and only reappeared in the 1980s. The reasons are discussed below. Most mainland Chinese studies of Xu Xu's work tend to focus on his prewar oeuvre.

2. For a brief discussion of these prewar and wartime works, see the Introduction. For a more in-depth analysis, see my two articles on the subject (Green 2011 and Green 2014). See also Christopher Rosenmeier's study that discusses some of Xu Xu's early works (Rosenmeier 2017).

3. Shi Huaichi was the pen name of Fudan University graduate Shu Yiren 束衣人. The essay quoted here is from an anthology of critical essays that was published posthumously and prefaced by Jin Yi 靳以 (1909-59), another prominent Marxist critic and writer.

4. Liu Yichang has remarked that most immigrant writers who wrote for the United States Information Service did so primarily for economic considerations since it was very difficult to make a living as a writer or intellectual in postwar Hong Kong (Liu 2002b, 203).

5. While some of Hesse's works were translated into Chinese in the 1920s and 1930s, Hesse was not a particularly influential author during the Republican period. Zhao Jingshen 趙景深 wrote articles about Hesse and translated some of his early short works into Chinese, which appeared in *The Short Story Magazine* 小說月報. *Siddhartha* did not appear in Chinese translation until 1974, when it was published in Taiwan as *Song of a Vagabond* 流浪者之歌, while *Steppenwolf,* which appeared the same year, was translated as *Wolf of the Steppes* 荒野之狼. Most Chinese scholarship on Hesse has since explored the influence Chinese thought has exerted on Hesse, and not vice-versa.

6. 《離魂》 (Lihun) has been translated into English by Eudora Yu as "Woman in the Mist." I am quoting from Yu's translation, but decided to render the title as "Departed Soul."

References

Ades, Dawn. 1994."Dada and Surrealism." In *Concepts of Modern Art: From Fauvism to Postmodernism*, edited by Nikos Stangos, 110-37. London: Thames and Hudson.

Berlin, Isaiah. 2009. *The Roots of Romanticism*. London: Chatto and Windus.

Boym, Svetlana. 2001. *The Future of Nostalgia*. New York: Basic Books.

Chan Chi-tak 陳智德. 2009. *Jieti wocheng: Xianggang wenxue, 1950-2005* 解體我城：香港文學, 1950-2005 [Dissecting my city: Hong Kong literature, 1950-2005]. Hong Kong: Huaqianshu Publishing.

Chipp, Herschel B. 1968. *Theories of Modern Art: A Source Book by Artists and Critics*. Berkeley: University of California Press.

Geng Chuanming 耿傳明. 2004. *Qingyi yu chenzhong zhi jian; 'Xiandai xing' wenti shiye zhong de 'xin langman pai' wenxue* 輕逸與沉重之間；「現代性」問題視野中的「新浪漫派」文學 [Between lightness and seriousness: "Romantic" literature and the problem of "Modernity"]. Tianjin: Nankai daxue chubanshe.

Goldman, Anne. 2008. "Soulful Modernism." *Southwest Review* 93.1, 13-30.

Green, Frederik H. 2011. "The Making of a Chinese Romantic: Cosmopolitan Nationalism and Lyrical Exoticism in Xu Xu's Early Travel Writings." *Modern Chinese Literature and Culture* 23.2, 64-99.

———. 2014. "Rescuing Love from the Nation: Love, Nation, and Self in Xu Xu's Alternative Wartime Fiction and Drama." *Frontiers of Literary Studies in China* 8.1, 126-53.

Hesse, Hermann. 1969. *The Journey to the East*, translated by Hilda Rosner. New York: Farrar, Strauss, and Giroux.

Kimmich, Anne 1936. *Kritische Auseinandersetzung mit dem Begriff*

Neuromantik in der Literaturgeschichtsschreibung [Critical analysis of the term neo-romanticism in literary history]. Tübingen: Albert Becht.

Kubin, Wolfgang. 2005. *Geschichte der chinesischen Literatur, Band 7. Die chinesische Literatur im 20. Jahrhundert* [History of Chinese literature, volume 7. Chinese literature during the 20th century]. München: K. G. Sauer.

Lee, Leo Ou-fan. 1973. *The Romantic Generation of Modern Chinese Writers.* Cambridge: Harvard University Press.

Leung, Ping Kwan. 2009. "Writing across Borders: Hong Kong's 1950s and the Present." In *Diasporic Histories: Cultural Archives of Chinese Transnationalism*, edited by Andrea Riemenschnitter and Deborah L. Madsen, 23–42. Hong Kong: Hong Kong University Press.

Liu Yichang 劉以鬯. 2002a. *Changtan Xianggang wenxue* 暢談香港文學 [Chats about Hong Kong literature]. Hong Kong: Holdery Publishing.

———, ed. 2002b. *Xianggang duanpian xiaoshuo xuan (wushi niandai)* 香港短篇小說選（五十年代）[Hong Kong short story collection (the 1950s)]. Hong Kong: Cosmos Books.

Lo Wai-luen 盧瑋鑾. 1998. "'Nanlai zuojia' qiantan" 「南來作家」淺談 [A few words about writers who came south]. In *Zhuiji Xianggang wenxue* 追跡香港文學 [In search of Hong Kong literature], edited by Huang Jichi 黃繼持, Lo Wai-luen 盧瑋鑾, and William Tay 鄭樹森, 113–24. Hong Kong: Oxford University Press.

Löwy, Michael. 2001. *Romanticism Against the Tide of Modernity*, translated by Robert Sayre and Catherine Porter. Durham, NC: Duke University Press.

Murong Yujun 慕容羽軍. 2003. "Xu Xu—Zuojia zhong de mingxing" 徐訏—作家中的明星 [Xu Xu: A star among writers]. *Xiangjiang wentan* 香江文壇 [Hong Kong's literary circle] 5.17, 15–19.

Rosenmeier, Christopher. 2017. *On the Margins of Modernism: Xu Xu, Wumingshi and Popular Chinese Literature in the 1940s.* Edinburgh: Edinburgh University Press.

Safransky, Rüdiger. 2007. *Romantik: Eine Deutsche Affäre* [Romanticism: A German affair]. München: Carl Hanser Verlag.

Schwede, Reinhild. 1987. *Wilhelminische Neuromantik. Flucht oder Zuflucht?* [Wilhelminian neo-romanticism. Escape or sanctuary?]. Frankfurt: Athenäum.

Shi Huaichi 石懷池. 1945. "Bangxian de mengyi 'Guilian'—Xu Xu de shu zhi yi" 幫閑的夢囈 《鬼戀》—徐訏的書之一 [The trashy rigmarole "Ghost love": One of Xu Xu's books]. In *Shi Huaichi wenxue lunwenji* 石懷池文學論文集 [Collection of essays on literature by Shi Huaichi], edited by Jin Yi 靳以, 151–54. Shanghai: Gengyun chubanshe.

Steiner, George. 1997. *Nostalgia for the Absolute*. New York: House of Anansi Press.

Wang Pu 王璞. 2003. *Yige gudu de jiang gushi ren—Xu Xu xiaoshuo yanjiu* 一個孤獨的講故事人—徐訏小說研究 [A lonely storyteller. Research on Xu Xu's fiction]. Hong Kong: Libo Publishing.

Wang Yixin 王一心. 1995. "Xu Xu yu Ba Ren de bimo guansi" 徐訏與巴人的筆墨官司 [Ba Ren and Xu Xu's battles of words]. *Shijie huawen wenxue luntan* 世界華文文學論壇 [Global Sinophone literature forum] 1, 65–67.

Xu Xu 徐訏. 1971. *Woman in the Mist*, translated by Eudora Yu. Hong Kong: Rainbow Press.

———. 1974. "Sister Tsui-ling," translated by George Kao. *Renditions* 2, 99–114.

———. 1991. "Xin gexing zhuyi wenyi yu dazhong wenyi" 新個性主義文藝與大眾文藝 [The literature and art of a new individualism and mass literature]. In *Xiandai Zhongguo wenxue guoyanlu* 現代中國文學過眼錄 [Taking a glance at modern Chinese literature], 267–84. Taipei: Shibao Publishing.

———. 2003. "Zhuisi Lin Yutang Xiansheng" 追思林語堂先生 [Recalling Lin Yutang]. In *Nianren yishi—Xu Xu yiwenxuan* 念人憶事—徐訏佚文選 [Remembrances: Obituaries by Xu Xu], edited by Liao Wenjie 廖文傑 and Wang Pu 王璞, 71–96. Hong Kong: Centre for Humanities Research, Lingnan University.

———. 2008. *Xu Xu wenji* 徐訏文集 [The collected works of Xu Xu], edited by Qian Zhenhua 錢震華. Volumes 1–16. Shanghai: Sanlian shudian.

Yan Jiayan 嚴家炎. 1986. *Zhongguo xiandai geliupai xiaoshuo xuan* 中國現代各流派小說選 [Anthology of works from the various modern Chinese literary groups]. Beijing: Beijing daxue chubanshe.

———. 1989. *Zhongguo xiandai xiaoshuo liupaishi* 中國現代小說流派史 [History of modern Chinese literary groups]. Beijing: Renmin wenxue chubanshe.

Yeh, Michelle. 2007. "'On our Destitute Dinner Table': *Modern Poetry Quarterly* in the 1950s." In *Writing Taiwan: A New Literary History*, edited by

David Der-Wei Wang and Carlos Rojas, 113–39. Durham, NC: Duke University Press.

Zhou Yang 周揚. 1996. "Thoughts on Realism," translated by Catherine Pease Campbell. In *Modern Chinese Literary Thought: Writings on Literature, 1893–1945*, edited by Kirk A. Denton, 335–44. Stanford, CA: Stanford University Press.

XU XU 徐訏 (1908–80) was an influential Chinese writer who enjoyed tremendous popularity from the late 1930s through the 1960s. After graduating from Peking University, he moved to Shanghai in 1933 to begin his literary career. He left for Paris in 1936 to continue his studies but soon returned to China after the outbreak of war with Japan. He emigrated to Hong Kong in 1950, where he continued to publish copious amounts of fiction, poetry, and literary criticism. Xu Xu's works were banned on the mainland from 1949 until the 1980s, but they are now widely read in China and are a frequent source of material for television and the stage. In Hong Kong, Xu Xu also edited several literary journals and taught Chinese literature at different colleges and universities, eventually chairing the Chinese Department at Hong Kong Baptist University until his death in 1980.

FREDERIK H. GREEN is associate professor of Chinese at San Francisco State University. He is the author of numerous articles and book chapters on the literature and culture of the Qing dynasty and the Republican period, Sino-Japanese cultural relations, post-socialist Chinese cinema, and contemporary Chinese art. He holds a BA in Chinese Studies from Cambridge University and an MPhil and PhD in Chinese literature from Yale University. He currently resides in San Francisco.